To Dad

The Suggestive Flyfisher

CONTENTS

**Published by Classic Trout Promotions,
P.O. Box 2459 Edenvale,
South Africa 1610.**

1st Edition 1987

*Other titles by Malcolm Meintjes
Trout on the Veld (1983)
Trout Trails of the Transvaal.*

ISBN 0-620-11855-5

CHAPTER 1

A Fascination with Flies

I've always been fascinated by flies. As a young boy I saw my first flybox being opened on the banks of a beautiful Kenya stream. The flies, so neatly arrayed, were "poisonous", I was told. And they looked deadly too, with their gleaming, sharpened hooks and their outward deception. That they looked like real flies, was the one thing I remember, and I was entranced by their names — Kenya Bug, Watson's Fancy, Coachman and Royal Coachman.

They were successful too, deceiving trout after trout, and though I did not fish, the part that these flies played in the seduction of the trout left a lasting impression.

Since then I've taken many trout on countless different flies. Enough, I suppose, to confuse anyone. Those early flies, I imagined, had a magic which made them irresistible. They truly looked as though they could exude poison. Then as the years passed and innumerable creations passed through my hands, it all became a practical endeavour. A cold calculating pursuit.

Even though it is clear that the angler's strategy is paramount in determining the catch, this book will endeavour to show that the fly is still important. Most flies will, it is true, catch trout at some time or another, but that is hardly the point. The angler is endeavouring to catch trout at one particular time and there is no doubt in my mind, that the way the angler uses his selection will, on the majority of occasions, bring him more success. To quote a well worn phrase: All flies are equal, but some are more equal than others. A Dragonfly nymph can be absolutely deadly, but not under all conditions.

We are often asked to choose between the importance of the fly and the importance of presentation, but is there any reason why we cannot consider both to be of value. Then too, I might argue, is the choice of fly not also a part of presentation?

The object of this book is to give some thought to the role the fly can play in our angling. These patterns all do catch fish, but if we use them with some thought and consideration they can be so much more deadly.

It has become fashionable to be disdainful of the older patterns yet, in doing so, we turn a blind eye to their credentials — credentials which go back, in many cases, over a hundred years or more.

Then there is the exciting world of imitative angling and the development of our own creative abilities on the flytying vice. If the fly was as unimportant as some would have us believe, would there be any point in developing new patterns?

I have lost count of the times I have been asked, "What fly should I tie on now?" Perhaps these all too few pages which follow, will give the reader some food for thought.

THE ROLE OF TRADITION

Trout fishing in South Africa has not really changed that much since the turn of the century. Certainly there are some anglers who have adopted new styles and fashions and there are indications that the up-and-coming generation may differ in thought, but on the whole the average South African trout fisher is conservative in outlook.

However, this conservativeness is not per se a bad thing. Trout fishing and the art of fly presentation is, by nature, not expected to change radically. The method of casting a fly is essentially primitive and the way in which it is performed today, is little different from the manner in which our forebears cast a fly. We do not wish it to change — it is part of a tradition and keeping within that tradition is one of the reasons that we enjoy flyfishing.

Once inside that orb of tradition, there is and has been, much turbulence. Different moralities have, throughout the centuries arisen, and as a result of what might seem to an outsider to be a mere storm in a teacup, incredible acrimony has resulted.

A FLY IS A FLY

One of the most enduring debates has encompassed the very definition of flyfishing. Today the "fly" is really regarded as any concoction of artificial materials tied on a hook. The originator of such a "fly" may consider it to be something that lives in, on, or around the waterside, or it may equally perplex him as to its identity. The point is that today's "flies" may not resemble natural flies (but frogs, tadpoles, forage fish, etc) and therefore, while strictly speaking to fish with such creations may still acceptedly be regarded as legal trout fishing, the inescapable logic is that it is not flyfishing.

A WIDER DEFINITION

While accepting the correctness of this argument, I do believe that the term "flyfishing" has become generic in nature over the years. Thus, the vast majority would still refer to a fellow angler as indulging in flyfishing, even should he be using a pattern simulating a small fish. One example of this generic use of the term, is "salmon fly". None of these gaudy apparitions was ever intended to vaguely resemble a natural fly, yet the term "salmon fly" has for many years been accepted.

RULES AND MORALS

Morality plays a major part in trout fishing. Select any specific topic and you'll be sure to be confronted with a diversity of opinions. Each protagonist will be equally dogmatic in presuming his point of view to be correct. I have no argument with any person who espouses a particular outlook, but equally that person has no right to castigate another for his approach. As long as the rules of the fishery are observed, each man to his own.

THE DRY FLY CODE

The problem with being morally righteous with others is that, with few exceptions, the particular brand of philosophy, if argued to its logical conclusion, can have flaws exposed. Take, for example, our original definition of flyfishing, ie. fishing with an imitation of a natural fly. The most persuasive argument was put forward by Frederic M. Halford who went one step further. It was not sufficient that one should fish with an artificial creation of any adult fly (whether in dun or spinner stage) but the artificial itself should be "dressed to imitate as faithfully as possible . . . (the natural fly)."

I believe that the disciples of Halford were more extreme in their interpretation of the Master's words and propounded the theory of the "perfect imitation". This latter theory, which felled all before it, later was turned inside out. No matter how "perfect" the imitation, there was never a natural fly which ever carried around with it a sharpened hook. Yet Halford did not even believe in accidental imitation and would not use the Gold Ribbed Hare's Ear, because he could not establish which particular fly it purported to imitate. To Halford, therefore, there was a distinguishable degree of imitation to make an artificial acceptable. The difficulty, however, is in determining a degree of imitation which separates that which is acceptable, from that which is not.

The Gold Ribbed Hare's Ear may have had all the standard attributes of a dry fly, but even though it looked like a dry fly, to Halford it was not a fly.

To digress for a moment, Halford has been labelled in derogatory terms as a "purist", but although it is said he became more dogmatic in his later years, the following passage belies this image as far as others were concerned:

Talking of so-called "fancy flies" — "If an experienced fisherman has implicit belief in the efficacy of a Wickham . . . (fancy fly) . . . he must add it to his list, because, as before said, nothing tends to success with a particular fly more surely than this implicit belief in its efficacy."

CHAPTER 2

Theories on Flies

THE OLD MASTERS

The success of various trout patterns has, through history, confounded re-searchers. Literally thousands upon thousands of patterns have been developed, yet relatively speaking, a handful have made it through the test of time. What is it that distinguishes these success stories from their brethren? The answer would have been easy if all the successful patterns had been "perfect imitations" but, as with the case of the G.R.H.E., there were many killing patterns, which seemingly had a low degree of imitation.

Francis Francis, one of the great anglers of the 19th century, although conceding that fancy flies could kill, said of the flyfisher:

"His art is unquestionably a deception and he must allow that he is deceiving the fish with an imitation of a fly . . . the better the imitation, the more likely it is to deceive."

Francis did not spurn the fancy fly, but cautioned that, before one turned to such creations, the angler should establish that which the trout might be feeding on and match that preference.

It seems clear that Francis believed that the factor of imitation (ie. likeness in overall form) was the catalyst that actually deceived the trout, but it is significant that his choice of words in the following passage encompassed a theory that only really became fashionable many years later:

"It is only because these combinations of fur and feather *in some sort,* resemble the flies they . . . (the trout) . . . are accustomed to seeing, that the trout take them at all."

Resemblance "in some sort" would certainly not have passed the Halford acid test of acceptability.

THE PRONOUNCEMENTS OF HALFORD

There is little doubt that F.M. Halford was one of the great Masters of the flyfishing world. His entomological endeavours to provide the concept of flyfishing with a logical base are astounding. Remember that Halford was a forerunner in his field, and one gets an inkling of the magnitude of his contribu-tion. For example, one of the greatest tasks confronting Halford was to find a method of preserving his natural fly specimens. Formulin was not yet on the market!

Halford concentrated on size and relative proportions of the natural fly in attempting imitation, but of paramount importance was colour. He recognised those times, when he doubted if a colour variation would affect the particular killing properties of a fly but added:

"At the same time, there are occasions when, and places where, one is almost tempted to think that the colour perception of the Salmonidae is developed to the highest degree."

Bear in mind that it is not too long ago that anglers were still arguing over the question of whether or not trout could see colour. Halford was not only convinced that they could, but seems to suggest that their perception of colour might even be more developed than that of the angler. The distinctions of shades that confronted Halford were so precise that they confounded description. Halford, in lieu thereof, published colour charts in his books to explain what he meant by a certain shade of colour. The raison d'etre of his book was to "reproduce in the artificial flies, the exact shades and tones of colour of the natural insects they are intended to counterfeit".

There are two interesting aspects of Halford's research. The first is that he always advocated collecting natural fly specimens from the water, not the bankside vegetation. The second is that he formulated no conclusion concerning species of natural fly, until he had collected at least 50 such specimens. This was so that any abnormal examples could be discarded. The standard patterns, he said, should imitate the *most plentiful* and therefore *normal* size, shape and colouring.

It is a touch ironic that much of Halford's work was done with the aid of G.S. Marryat, who once drew attention to "the importance of the 'driver' ".

THE CONTRIBUTION OF SKUES

Almost in the same breath as Halford comes the contribution of George Edward Mackenzie Skues. The work of Halford and Skues concerning dry fly and nymph fishing respectively was remarkable and one is astounded at the bitterness of the controversial debate that was to follow.

Whereas Halford looked to close imitation as a basis for flyfishing, Skues postulated that imitation, representation and suggestion of the trout's natural food would be acceptable. However, he maintained that these had to be fished "in the conditions in which the trout is feeding" . . . (on the natural food).

"Matching the hatch" was not to be neglected and he stated, in his experience on the chalk streams, that one fly would not do as well as another. The trout, on many occasions, would, for some reason, refuse all but one pattern which, during that particular period, would appear *to them (the trout)* to be the natural fly on which they were feeding.

It is significant to note that Skues was postulating the proposition that trout might not see objects as an angler would. Of examples given, one was that old mystery of why a trout should readily accept a Gold Ribbed Hare's Ear, when the large spring medium olive dun was hatching. These instances Skues termed "unlike likeness".

Thus the logic of the dry fly purist began to founder. If the quest for precise imitation should lead to greater efficacy, the examples of the "unlike likeness" should not occur with such regularity.

The commonest imitation which catches most fish, said Skues, is caricature. A definition of caricature is: Grotesque representation . . . by over-emphasis on characteristics.

SAWYER AND KITE

During the fifties and sixties, two more acknowledged authorities on nymph fishing emerged along the banks of the English chalk streams. They were respectively Frank Sawyer and Major O.W.A. Kite.

Frank Sawyer, keeper for many years of a stretch of the Upper Avon, met Skues for the first time in 1945. At that meeting Skues was 90 years of age, but had lost little of his remarkable insight. He was so impressed with Sawyer that he was prepared to write to A. and C. Black to ask them to keep an eye on this "angling writer of exceptional promise". While Sawyer's work on nymph fishing became classic in its own right, it complemented that of Skues, for while the latter concentrated on fishing the nymph just under surface, Sawyer developed deeper water techniques. In doing so he originated what was to become the Netheravon style, which has also been called — the "induced take".

Sawyer began to move away from the ultra-imitation theory and pursued simplicity instead. Halford's search for imitation led him to list the "Hundred Best Patterns of Dry Flies" (later condensed to thirty-three) but even Skues' presentation of fifteen patterns was too many. Perhaps, concluded Sawyer, such creations should not be looked at from the angler's point of view, but from that of the fish.

To Sawyer, the joy in trout fishing came with the knowledge that one had deceived the trout into taking an imitation of the natural insect on which the fish were feeding. It was not enough however, to have a good copy, for it was the action of the artificial nymph which was the attraction.

One should bear in mind that Sawyer prefaces his remarks by confining them to a particular period during the season (following mid-summer) and considering only the natural insects which may be a source of trout food during this time.

Sawyer's learning process included being obsessed with tying exact imitations, which later were scaled down to ten patterns, all varying in size and colour. It became apparent that some were better than others and, in the following elimination process, three patterns evolved. In time, two of these patterns became one, christened the Grey Goose; the remaining one became known as Sawyer's pheasant tail nymph.

It became clear that Sawyer concentrated on producing, in one fly, a blend of dressing which would bring about a general representation of a number of different natural nymphs.

Of the importance of colour which Halford had so faithfully tried to capture, and which Skues had been tempted by logic alone to explore, Sawyer was convinced. He had concluded years before that trout saw colour in a fashion differently to humans. For example the rusty red of the pheasant tail body was taken readily when fish were feeding on nymphs of olive or greenish yellow hue.

Oliver Kite went further than Sawyer in some respects. The superficial external appearance of a nymph was only partly responsible for the trout's reaction to it. Like Sawyer, he stressed the manner in which the artificial had to be fished. Consideration had thus to be given to the study of the habits of the natural nymphs and the simulation of their movement.

Kite had no objection to the use of the more familiar wet fly patterns being fished selectively in the manner of nymphs, as he felt that many of them had been created, perhaps even subconsciously, as nymphal representations.

Later Kite said " . . . Pattern plays little part in nymph fishing as I understand it." Indeed he created the "bare hook" nymph with which he caught many grayling.

A STOP FOR A BREATHER

I believe it is necessary to remind the reader of some aspects which might have been overlooked. The above writers formulated many of their thoughts on the slow meandering chalk streams of England. Their considerations are not therefore finely tuned to still-water, nor, perhaps to rough-and-tumble streams or rivers which are not crystal clear.

The ethic of the day was upstream fishing, be it with nymph or dry fly and on these chalk streams it was not a matter of casting indiscriminately, but of spotting, stalking and fishing to a particular fish.

A second point which should be tucked away is that Halford's preoccupation with dry fly fishing and a high degree of imitation was developed with the characteristics of the chalk stream in mind. Obviously his mode of fishing precluded the dimension of depth and, to an overwhelming degree therefore, movement of an induced nature. Whereas Kite and Sawyer could impart action to the ascending nymph, Halford and, to a lesser extent Skues, had to rely on imitation to fool the trout.

MODERN STILLWATER THOUGHTS

In fishing any running water, slow or fast, with a sunken fly, there is always a certain amount of natural movement imparted to the fly. Indeed, even in "stillwater", there is nevertheless natural movement, which can be occasioned by wind action. However, in the main, the action of the fly past a trout, has to be instigated by the angler and, of course, the element of depth has more seriously to be considered.

Although stillwater fishing was not previously unknown in England, it was the opening of the big reservoirs such as Grafham in the Sixties, that started off a stillwater flyfishing boom. It became apparent to those who had been weaned on rivers and streams that this was a completely new animal, which had to be approached differently. New theories were put forward and certainly a host of new flies.

A LOOK AT IVENS

T.C. Ivens was probably the forerunner of the latter-day stillwater angler and he was instrumental in moving towards a more imitative approach, even though his patterns could not be construed as being highly imitative. Until then, the vast majority of artificials used on stillwater trout were no more than a gathering of salmon patterns — or "lures" as some preferred to call them.

Another element had however begun to creep in. To a great extent flyfishing, in its purest sense, had been about imitation. In other words, if a pattern was imitative of a natural fly it was a fly; if not, then it was heaven-knows-what. As more and more reservoir anglers appeared on the scene, research showed that these trout fed on more than just hatches of natural fly. An equally impressive school of "perfect imitation" theorists was to come into being. The only problem was, they were not imitating flies but other aquatic creatures, such as shrimps, snail, small fish, etc.

It was an interesting anomaly. We had angling with a high degree of imitation which was not considered flyfishing; and we had vague impersonation which was.

. . . GODDARD . . .

In the meantime angler-entomologist John Goddard had done some sterling work in the stillwater fly recognition field and had put forward some patterns of use, but he made no distinction between flies and non-flies.

There seemed to be an implied acceptance of a wider definition of flyfishing. Even though one fished with a perfect imitation of a shrimp, could this strictly be called "flyfishing?" No, said Conrad Voss Bark. "A fly is a fly."

. . . VOSS BARK . . .

Voss Bark's initial approach confined itself to nymph fishing for lake trout with suggestions, not imitations, primarily of the lake and pond olive. That his nymphal suggestions could be taken by the trout for another insect species, was within contemplation, and herein lies an enigma. Voss Bark favoured the palmer dressing of flies, a practice which he regarded as enhancing the versatility of a pattern. So versatile that he quotes Courtney Williams as maintaining that such a pattern, thinly dressed, could be taken for a shrimp, nymph or a number of different types of larvae. Presumably then if the trout took the artificial for a nymph or larvae, this would be considered flyfishing, if it took the same artificial for a shrimp, this would not be flyfishing.

Does it really follow, for there are not a few examples of this, as we shall see. It has been conceded that an artificial can resemble more than one natural fly and it is now proposed that some artificials can resemble vastly different creatures, fished by different anglers as suggestions of those different beings, and taken by the trout as . . . ?

Conrad Voss Bark did make two other points though. It was, he said, movement that attracted the fish and he suggested that the size of the fly was more important than colour.

THE ERA OF THE LURE

During the 1960s the advent of the stillwater fishing boom produced hordes of "lures" of virtually every conceivable shape and size. Trout snapped up these colourful apparitions to the constant surprise of most and theories on trout aggression were formulated.

Far from being revolutionary, the conclusions drawn merely confirmed that which had been known for many years, and had indeed been commented upon by Skues, namely, that trout would take an artificial without any feeding motive being present.

Although stillwater flyfishing had been practised for many years, the role of imitation and suggestion in the relevant flies was not appreciated by the majority of anglers until years later. In fact, unjustifiably, stillwater trout fishing was viewed for some time as a chuck-and-chance-it affair using salmon patterns. It was probable that a basic misconception about the trout's feeding habits in dams and lakes simply engendered generations of fry imitating lures.

Only once sufficient stomach content analysis had been done, was it appreciated that small fry made up a relatively insignificant proportion of the trout's diet. It came as a revelation to some, that flyfishing in the purest sense could still be practised.

Such was the message of Conrad Voss Bark.

Even so, few anglers were prepared to restrict the definition of flyfishing and consequently imitations and suggestions of non-flies such as frogs, crabs, snail and shrimps began to appear as part of the overall definition.

ON TO CLARKE

Brian Clarke attempted an overall analysis of the scene in the mid-seventies as it pertained to stillwater. The traditional flies, he said, fell into two basic categories. There was the "large lure" group such as the Alexandra and King-fisher Butcher and there were those which under certain circumstances could represent certain types of food. Seeking for a logical basis upon which to justify flyfishing, Clarke argued for a more imitative approach along the lines of "if the trout will accept a 'maybe' pattern, surely they would queue up for a 'sure fire' pattern."

Surprisingly though, Clarke brought up what he called "calculated suggestion" as an avenue to be explored. This comprised producing a suggestion of something, which even though it may not exist, nevertheless looks as though it should.

CHAPTER 3

The South African Connection

From the preceding pages it is clear that I have concentrated on the thoughts of English writers past and present. The reason for this is simply that much of the South African heritage has been forged along precisely the same lines. The older generation of flyfishers who angled in the Twenties and Thirties had been brought up on a diet of Halford and Skues. Such American influence as there has been, is relatively limited and, strangely enough, there are probably more New Zealand flies present than one would have thought.

It is therefore not surprising that the limited literary debates that have taken place in South Africa have followed either the exact imitation or presentation theories. Since the exact imitation cult belonged more precisely to a chalk stream environment, the "it's not what you fish, but how you fish it" brigade has largely ruled the roost.

This attitude is plainly evident in the process involved in choosing a fly. Come hell or high water, the first fly on has got to be a Walkers Killer and that we'll flog for a good four hours before a radical change is instituted and a Mrs Simpson is stuck on. If no success occurs, it's clear that the trout are "off" and it's a toss up between a Connemara Black, Invicta, Red Setter (sunny day) or back to the Walkers Killer.

I'm not being funny or derogatory when I say this, for the basic philosophy being espoused is that the pattern is essentially unimportant and that presentation is paramount. Yet at the same time, certain patterns are regarded as better than others.

BOWKER AND OTHERS

One of South Africa's most outspoken writers was adamant on this subject. Fred Bowker ("Kingfisher") who was noted for his catches on the Eerste River (Cape) was in no doubt whatsoever that presentation was really all that counted. Bowker although born in England, had little experience of fishing in that country and came to South Africa in 1902. He made it clear that he did not consider dry fly fishing, a "greater art". Yet the same time, he considered that fishing "wet" (which he practised) was not flyfishing at all and should be called nymph or larvae fishing or possibly even lure fishing.

Bowker used four patterns — Claret and Mallard, March Brown (silver), Durham Ranger and Silver Wilkinson — but believed that any other quartet would be equally successful. The need for exact imitation was countered by the fact that good catches were made on creations that looked like "nothing on earth".

Bowker continues to pursue his case more on the basis of casting doubt on his adversaries' approach, than on proving his own. For example, he pointed out, the stomach contents of a trout did not prove that a trout would not have taken something else. Then too, he would argue, even though a trout did take your March Brown, are you sure it would not have been caught had you been using a Claret and Mallard?

"Kingfisher" went one step further. He later fashioned a fly deliberately using colours (pink and blue) that were "unfishy" and fished with the, then named, Mountain Swallow for a whole season.

Of course, Bowker's theories were not shared universally. Arthur H. Reid postulated a more imitative approach; Nuttall logically believed that there were occasions when trout would take anything and other times when they would discriminate.

Of the present South African authorities, not too detailed accounts have taken place and, in some cases, I would hesitate to relate that which has been written as an authoritative summary of the author's thoughts.

Tom Sutcliffe in a series of short articles, attributes to the trout an element of selectivity and preference, eg. trout would prefer to take flying ants than mayflies during a simultaneous hatch. In such situations the size, colour and behaviour of the natural should be considered. Later he goes on to say that the attributes which make up a good fly should be an element of suggestion, movement, appropriate fishing strategy and the artificial's materials should be made up of soft rather than rigid elements. The ability to create translucence, or what he calls, "a halo effect", increase the desirability of a fly. (Lesser anglers achieve this "halo effect" by grinding the fly into the mud with the heel of a boot).

Jack Blackman does not follow the exact imitation school, but suggests that colour and movement are important. He does however maintain that one should observe the lake bottom and match the colour of the fly to that particular area. (Perhaps one might call this "matching the patch").

On to Bob Crass, who is sceptical again of exact imitation, primarily because he believes it probable that the trout reacts more to a releaser than to detailed structure. To a great extent, Dr. Crass confirms the importance of size, shape, colour, texture and the floating or sinking properties of the fly, but says that minor colour differences are not significant. A rule of thumb is "Bright day — dark fly; dull day — red fly".

At present there is something of a revival in the art of fly tying, which in turn has promoted more thought towards those characteristics which a trout fly should encapsulate. On the other hand, the majority of South African flyfishers have preferred to remain faithful to many of the traditional patterns.

CHAPTER 4

Fact or Fallacy

It is common for trout anglers to fall into one or other School of Thought. One is either for or against. Each argument is usually argued quite logically and in those cases where logic is defeated, the irrationality of the trout is usually blamed.

Then too some of the arguments become over-complicated. Terminology becomes so precise that we eventually have no idea of what is going on. In some cases terminology is given two totally different meanings, in other cases there is an overlap of meaning.

Who can say when imitation ends and where suggestion begins?

At the risk of being technically incorrect, I have always preferred to use the words imitation and suggestion as referring respectively to:
— likeness in form;
— likeness in movement.

If this definition is accepted we would have artificials which have different degrees of imitation. A fly may be highly imitative or have little imitative appeal, but there is some element of imitation. This rules out an arbitrary assessment of the dividing line between imitation and non-imitation.

I also believe that if one sticks to the abovementioned definition, a number of distortions become clearer. An analysis of the aforementioned writers must surely have triggered some anomalies, the greatest being the apparent inexplicability of the success of the so-called traditional patterns. The other problem is that the degree of imitation lies in the eye of the beholder. I will give you one example close to home.

The Walkers Killer, probably South Africa's most popular fly, has been regarded by different anglers as resembling vastly differing creatures. To some it resembles a small Rana frog; to others a crab and even a dragonfly larva or nymph. Lionel Walker, himself, in an article about the fly alluded to its versatility.

Thus, depending on one's own perception, a pattern could have little appeal if viewed as a "frog", but a high degree of imitation if seen as a dragonfly larva. Not only therefore, would there be confusion as to whether the pattern is imitative or not, but controversy in the purist sense could reign. If the trout took the "fly" as a frog imitation this would not be flyfishing; if it mistook it for a dragonfly nymph it would be.

A pity we cannot refer to the fish for clarification.

CHAPTER 5

Traditional Patterns and their Counterparts

I t appears quite clear, notwithstanding the reasoning of the near imitation school, that the mystery of the success of the "traditional" patterns is easy to explain.

THE TEST OF TIME

No matter what "logic" is put forward, the majority of these patterns are supremely successful in practice and, what is more, they have stood the test of time. Their success, therefore, cannot simply be attributed to good fortune, nor, for that matter, constant usage.

What seems to have been overlooked by a number of writers is that (i) the trout's view of the fly may not be the same as the angler's; and (ii) that these flies, by accident or design, do have characteristics of the natural aquatic creatures incorporated into their make up. What is more, properly tied, the lack of near imitation is more than offset by their qualities of movement (suggestion).

A TROUT'S VIEW

The trout's view of the fly, overlooked by some, has been commented on by others. In most cases, a fair amount of guesswork as to that which the trout actually sees, has taken place. It is however worth noting, that the different medium in which the trout lives may very well alter perceptions of colour.

In the angler's case, his attempt at matching a particular colour, is usually done with dry materials. The mere wetting of the fly will change the shade, usually making it darker.

The trout, of course, may be looking at the fly through peat-stained or murky water and he may view the fly from a different angle.

For example, on a bright day, a trout looking to the surface for food and perhaps into the sun spots, what is to him, a black fly. He engulfs it, because it appears to have the outline of a creature that he is familiar with and which moves in an alluring fashion. The trout angler is amazed that the trout took his yellow Invicta. Against a very bright background one sometimes cannot distinguish colour. In addition, while form is important the trout is not used to seeing his prey always in a clear image. In a ripple, the best imitation may look disjointed and confused. Any advantage it may have had on the flytying vice could conceivably be lost, when placed in the water.

A further doubt is placed on the trout's perception of imitation and non-imitation by the proposition that no matter how well a fly is tied, the trout cannot fail to see the hook and the barb. Is it possible that the fish can miss the knot and length of nylon attached to the head of the fly? Perhaps the counter is that the trout simply attaches no significance to such apparitions. If so, one must place a question mark against some of the theories concerning trout behaviour that are put forward. If it makes little difference to a trout that a palpably unnatural hook is attached to the artificial, then would it really make any great difference to the trout whether the fly was a perfect imitation or not? Strictly speaking, only perhaps in the case of the dry fly, could a case for imitation be made as the hook is, to a degree, disguised by a film of water and the leader attachment is actually outside of the trout's environment.

Thus one view proposes that trout do not link hook nor tippet to danger. They do not say "Ah there is a cunningly disguised hook." They simply do not have such precise reasoning power.

A counter argument could well be that the trout is aware of hook and tippet and where its vision is not impaired, it is consequently very difficult to catch. One can identify with this proposition, for in a flat calm, where there is minimal fragmentation of image, anglers are usually found praying for a breath of wind.

TRADITIONAL PATTERNS — ACCIDENT OR DESIGN

Let us now take a look at the background of some of the traditional patterns that South Africans have for years been carrying around their flyboxes.

Many of the patterns mentioned below were first tied over a century ago and are certainly no strangers to our trout, yet the question of that which they and others purport to represent is still to be answered. Upon analysis of various writers, the following similarities were observed, some of which could be said to be somewhat surprising. However, the interesting point is that by purposefully using traditional patterns an angler could employ a wide range of imitative tactics.

	Fly	Representative of:
1.	Coch-y-bonddhu	Beetle, snail.
2.	Invicta	Sedge pupa, small perch.
3.	Butcher	Small fish, larva/nymph assortment, beetle.
4.	Greenwells Glory	Olive nymph.
5.	Pheasant tail nymph (Sawyer)	Olive nymph, shrimp.
6.	Peter Ross	Shrimp, bloodworm.
7.	Wickhams Fancy	Sedge.
8.	Zulu	Smut, assorted nymphs.
9.	Alexandra	Minnow, beetle.
10.	Coachman	Sedge, snail.
11.	March Brown	Small frog, gillieminkie, stonefly creeper.
12.	Black Gnat	Corixa, midge pupa.
13.	Connemara Black	Midge pupa.
14.	Royal Coachman	Bloodworm.
15.	Red Setter	Daphnia, ova.
16.	Walkers Killer	Dragonfly larva and nymph, Rana frog, crab.
16a.	Walkers nymph	Damselfly nymph, caenis nymph.
17.	Mrs Simpson	Dragonfly larva and nymph.

18.	Hamills Killer	Dragonfly larva and nymph.
19.	Baby Doll	Fry, phantom larva.
20.	Woolly Worm	Assorted nymphs.
21.	Muddler Minnow	Minnow, grasshopper, frog, damselfly nymph.
22.	Tups Indispensable	Caenis, midge.
23.	D.D.D.	Assorted terrestrials.
24.	Irresistible	Mayfly, sedge.
25.	Pheasant Tail Nymph (Cove)	Midge pupa, damselfly nymph.

Two noteworthy points can be made from the above list. Firstly, it would seem that some flies that look totally unlike one another, apparently, in some persons' imaginations, purport to imitate the same aquatic creature, eg. Alexandra and Coch-y-bonddhu. One might consider that the similarity comes into play in the water, ie. they are probably more suggestive than imitative.

The second point is that certain aquatic creatures lend themselves to imitation. For example, sedges apparently can be represented by Invicta, Wickhams Fancy, Coachman and Irresistible.

CONCLUSION

One tends to get the impression in examining certain writers, that we should move away from the traditional patterns towards a more imitative approach. Again I question the rationale behind this and wonder why one should be asked to opt for an "either-or" situation. What logic makes the Peacock Woolly Worm "in" and the Walkers Killer "out"? The Walkers Killer, as we have seen, has much to commend it. It has more releasers than some so-called imitative flies I have seen. Imitative fishing is fun and I would recommend it, but its allure lies, not in the denigration of the traditional patterns, but in its own contribution to fly fishing.

Certainly, we have seen the emergence of some dubious apparitions, some of which are extremely modern and whose chief object is to goad an already aggressive trout into striking, but I believe, as has been demonstrated, that many of our traditional patterns have imitative and multi-imitative characteristics and since they have stood the test of time, should be accorded the respect they deserve.

Perhaps it is a romantic notion, but one day soon, I am going to take my split cane rod out of its bag and accompanied by Coachman, Royal Coachman, Butchers et al saunter down to the river to enjoy my fishing.

A fine specimen of a Rainbow trout cockfish - 8 lb. 10 oz.

Brown trout taken by author on a Natal dam - 4½ lb.

Success on the Lunsklip (E. Transvaal)

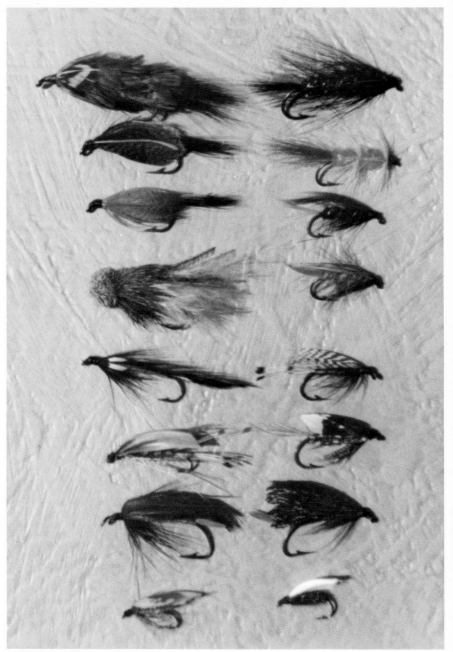

L.H.S.: Mrs. Simpson, Walker's Killer, Hamill's Killer, Muddler Minnow (var.), Walker's Black Widow, Hardy's Favourite, Butcher, March Brown.

R.H.S.: Peacock Woolly Worm, Red Setter, Connemara Black, Invicta, Peter Ross, Jock Scott, Alexandra (Green), Coachman.

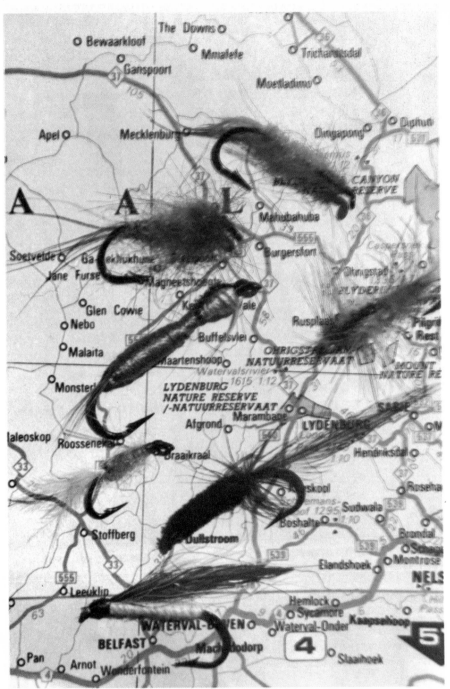

From top to bottom: Diggers Red, Malcolm's Joseph, Kering'ende nymph, Aberdare nymph, Plewman's Killer, Tadpole, Bourke's Luck.

Marrow spooning indicates heavy feeding on daphnia.

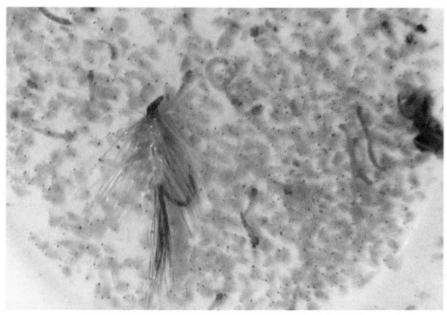

Daphnia close up showing rusty tinge and Red Setter.

Dragonfly nymphs.

Damselfly nymphs

Choked to the gills

Bloodworm (midge larvae)

23

Corixa

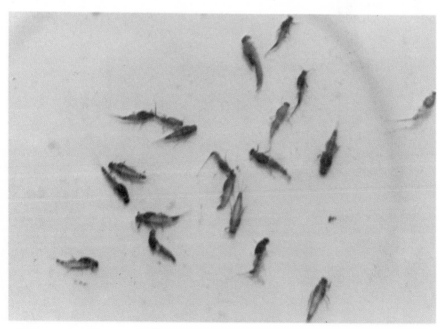

The Angler's Curse - caenis

Small Barbus and snails

A mixture of terrestrials, midge pupae and larvae, snail, caenis.

Another pot-pourri - dragonfly nymph and larvae, damselfly nymph, corixa etc.

From minute to a mouthful

27

Tranquility and a Brown trout for John Webber.

The author with a trio of 3 lb. Rainbows taken off the top.

CHAPTER 6

Entomology

THE DEGREE OF PRECISENESS?

If one accepts the argument that precise and accurate imitation is not an absolute prerequisite to success, then it also follows that precise and absolute knowledge of entomology is also not required. Most people are switched off by the seemingly ultra-scientific process that goes into identifying the Hylobatinae subfamily as opposed to Pongo pygmaeus.

Essentially the degree of knowledge required is that which will allow one to recognise, in a general fashion, that which the trout are likely to be feeding on, eg, dragonfly nymph and thereafter to imitate it in an appropriately suggestive fashion.

The problem is that, since most flyfishers do not involve themselves with stomach contents analysis, they would not be able to recognise the aquatic dolly mixture.

PRACTICALITIES BEFORE SCIENCE

I would therefore prefer to adopt a practical approach and concentrate on those food items which are most commonly found in stomach contents. Perhaps, as in the case of the trout, we should dwell on overall form and then identify characteristics of the aquatic insect to make recognition easier. In this way, the newcomer to entomology will recognise midge pupa without being confused about pinpointing its precise location in the family tree. After all, in practice, prompt identification, even in a general sense, is not always that easy because of the digestive process and detritus that accompanies such findings. Indeed it can be downright difficult to identify precisely the various nymphs, pupae and larvae that will be found. Even general identification of these minute creatures will not be easy.

So let's do things differently and look at some examples of that which we might find in a trout's stomach. Before we begin, however, a couple of useful accompaniments are suggested. Get yourself the inappropriately named "marrow spoon" and a dish or saucer in which to place the stomach contents.

CAUTION IN CONCLUSIONS

Fred Bowker was not at all impressed by the process of stomach contents analysis. The fact that a trout had been feeding on certain items did not mean they would refuse something else. And if the "something else" was an artificial fished appropriately, then it made nonsense of the so-called selectivity of trout.

There are a number of reasons why Bowker's flies could have been successful. The most obvious is that they could easily have induced an aggressive reaction which does not rely on the feeding motive at all, or it may have been that those flies nevertheless incorporated some "releasers" within their make-up which the trout recognised.

Be that as it may, I have always considered that some information is better than none and if one does have an idea of what the trout have been feeding on, in many instances, this information can be put to good use.

However I agree with Bowker that stomach contents can be misleading. Most anglers gut their fish some time after capture and in so doing have a cursory peep at the contents. This, of course, will show what the trout have been feeding on, but it will not tell them what the fish were preoccupied with at that particular time. A nice fat dragonfly nymph may emerge from the stomach, but it is probable that the nymph was taken some hours earlier and perhaps not in the same vicinity.

By rights one should spoon the fish first and observe thereby the latest delicacies. Make a mental note of the order and then place the contents in a saucer of water. The saucer will (i) establish perhaps that some of the nymphs, larvae, etc, are still alive which should indicate time of feeding; and (ii) sort out the various aquatic creatures properly. When one has a marrow spoon stuffed to the hilt with hundreds of little creatures, a grubby finger poking through the assembly will not be sufficient to assist recognition.

It's also true that we look, but we do not see. Make a note of the colour of the nymphs and larvae. It's easy to miss the pale colours that many of these creatures are made up off. For example what may seem black at first sight could actually be dark brown. I can also promise you that nature's subtle use of colour will astound you.

Once we have been through with the marrow spoon, then it is a good idea to clean the fish and analyse further down what is present. These contents may confirm the feeding preference, but they may also show a complete change in behaviour.

In some examinations the marrow spoon may indicate relatively little, but it's worthwhile to take a good look, because you may have been fortunate enough to hook a fish prior to a feeding splurge and the one or two seemingly insignificant specimens will be worth their weight in gold.

Stomach contents would also seem to indicate that trout can be highly selective. The composition of such contents can be made up almost totally of one particular foodsort. Yet selectivity does not always mean that the trout will be that difficult to catch. Trout can be selective on the surface or selective deeper down. Selectivity on the surface can be a problem, tactically speaking, because of the number (and often, size) of the foodsort, but a bigger practical problem is that the trout's window is small because he is close to the surface. He simply may not see your fly.

Selectivity deeper down is only a problem if one is not aware of the foodsort. Here the trout will take your fly — if it has the right characteristics. But remember too that, because such feeding may be localised, your strategic approach is paramount, eg. are you fishing at the right level or where the activity is taking place?

The stomach contents can give a clue here too. Is the foodsort indicative of that on the surface or is it lower down? Is there weed or mud mixed in with the contents? And finally try to match those findings with whatever other information you have, eg. the method used to catch that trout or "rise forms" taking place.

There are still many anomalies which will, on countless occasions, disregard any general rules that one might fashion. There have been days when I have struggled to catch a trout and have pondered whether they are totally off the feed. A chance capture however confirms heavy feeding. On other occasions trout after trout have been hooked and the majority have had iron hard stomachs with nothing in them.

Then again, many days have been saved when the stomach contents draw the veil, the right fly has been selected and the tactic has worked like a charm.

CHAPTER 7

Deliberate Imitation and Suggestion

LIMITATIONS OF THE TRADITIONALS

We have previously mentioned the role that traditional flies can play in imitative angling. While there is much scope, it is also true that there are limitations to this approach. Although I believe that the originators of these flies probably had an idea of what their flies represented, it must also be acknowledged that many of these flies are not, today, tied with the same materials nor care that is often required. Such deviations in tying undoubtedly will have an effect on the efficacy of the fly. From a personal point of view, I know how particular I can be on the tying of some of my patterns. The colour has to be just right, the shape just so and, in the water, the overall impression of form and movement must be correct. Sometimes if these elements are not in order, I lose faith in that particular creation. If the originator of a fly needs those elements to ensure a high degree of success, how difficult it must be for a commercial tyer to emulate this "precision".

SATISFACTION IN FLY TYING

There is a tremendous amount of satisfaction derived from tying one's own flies and it is unfortunate that more anglers do not persevere with this sideline. More precisely, the tying up of a fly with a certain strategy in mind is fulfilling and from a practical point of view, it does open many more options. I personally like the "caricature" approach and there are many permutations in nature which make the whole aspect of fly tying worthwhile considering. During the season, one may find dragonfly nymphs of various shades of colour and an assortment of sizes. It is impractical to try and match these permutations in ready-made form and so the accompaniment of the fly tying outfit does give one a bankside advantage as well as being extremely good fun.

If one simply matches the size of flies generally used by anglers, to the stomach contents of most trout, it immediately becomes apparent that 90% of the things trout feed on are not just tiny, but miniscule in comparison. The visibility of the fly is important, but I sometimes think that the confidence of anglers increases with *their* ability to see the fly, rather than the trout's ability.

FLY TYING CONSIDERATIONS

For those who are prepared to dabble in tying up flies let us review some of the more common attributes which a fly might incorporate into its make-up. We have seen that flyfishers are by no means universal in their opinions of why some flies are successful and certainly through the years, particular emphasis has been laid on some aspects to the possible detriment of others.

Each fly tyer will have to decide which style will suit him better and which features he is going to concentrate on.

THE IMPORTANCE OF COLOUR

In analysing the various attitudes concerning colour that I have heard over the last few years, I have come to the conclusion that many people no longer consider colour to be important. Now, in saying this, I do not mean that anglers are insensitive to colour changes as a whole, but relatively little attention is paid to different shades of the same colour or to a mixture of various shades and colours.

Cognisance should be taken of the fact that trout are at much closer range to the fly than we are. Pick up most flies and ask an angler what colours are incorporated therein and it's a certainty that he will immediately pick out the primary colours and, thereafter with differing degrees of difficulty, he will list the other colours in general terms. Put the fly under a microscope and it will be apparent how little colour we actually appreciate.

It matters not what theory we tend to follow, for it could well be, in either case, that colour as an "imitator" or "releaser" is a very strong catalyst in persuading a trout to take hold of the fly.

As we have seen, one of the proponents of the importance of colour was Halford. He was of the opinion that trout had an extremely high degree of perception when it came to colour and, indeed, since Halford found it impossible to describe the various shades involved, he incorporated a colour chart into his writings so that readers would visually be able to correspond with his comments. There were times, he said, when it seemed as though the colour perception of the trout was developed "to the highest degree". It was quite clear that Halford attached much importance to exact shade and tone of colour which had to be imitated.

This opinion was shared by G.E.M. Skues and subsequent writers, but while they list colour as being important, one does sense that they are not referring to colour with the same precision as did Halford. An exception to this was James "Invicta" Ogden whose fly creating abilities should not be underestimated. Indeed Ogden believed that colour involved such subtlety that shade differences, seen only under a magnifying glass, could neverthe-less make the difference. "Colour," he said "is a grand secret in fly tying."

Richard Walker alluded to the presence of key colours which were apparent in natural insects and regarded the incorporation of a key colour in an artificial as a step towards making it significantly more attractive. For example, in the Olives, chestnut was a key colour and in the Pond Olive, light orange or apricot. This matched the belief of Halford/Skues who used tying silk in appropriate colours to match the "keys". For instance, the Iron Blue incorporated crimson silk, while hot orange silk was used to tie up the Blue Winged Olive.

Walker, Goddard and Clarke all considered the trout's ability to see colour. Trout were able to see colour as distinctly as humans could and possibly even deeper into the infra-red. From experiments conducted, it appeared that fish see red, orange and yellow most easily, but two points emerged that were of interest:

1) A colour easily seen did not necessarily indicate that the trout would take flies incorporating those colours in preference to others;

nor

2) Did trout necessarily see colours as we see them.

Walker in fact did point out certain anomalies. We have mentioned, above, the key colour orange, in relation to the B.W.O. Skues found that when trout were feeding on blue winged olives, the Orange Quill was a successful fly to use. Another case is given where trout feeding on the crane fly, react less favourably to the highly imitative brown artificial than to a bright green. The question begs itself: Does a trout "see" brown as bright green or is there a hidden "key" colour (bright green) which the trout can see, which we cannot?

Let me give you a personal inference of a key colour's importance in modern stillwater flyfishing theory. It has been known for some time that when daphnia are in abundance, particularly near the surface, that a fly incorporating orange (or hot orange) is extremely useful. The reason for this preference was not so well known, but I mentioned in "Trout on the Veld" that once, while holding a plastic bag full of daphnia, I noticed an overall impression of a rusty brown/orange colour. I suggested that this could be the link. In Church and Gathercole's new book, an excellent close up of a single daphnia confirmed the delicate "rusty" hue, which to the naked eye is not visible. Then too are you aware of that little grey fly called the caenis? Well, it's not grey at all, but its body hues are pale yellow and brown.

Another extremely interesting aspect of colour importance is brought up by Walker. One would consider that the incorporation of a key colour, to be attractive to the fish, would have to be positioned correctly in the fly. The female sedge has a yellow sac at the tail-end of its body. Walker's imitation follows this positioning, but Lunn's Caperer has a yellow band in the centre of the body. Walker also suggests that Ivens' imitation of a sedge pupa has the key colours the wrong way round, yet it remains a killer pattern.

I believe that certain of the theories have edged nearer to a possibility not fully explored, but seemingly logical. It seems to me that the undoubted success of the caricature (releaser) theory and its widespread popularity has lead to an acceptance that trout recognise a particular characteristic of the natural in a fly. So, traditionally, we tie up the imitation and, to give it more allure, incorporate and exaggerate the recognition point. But what if the trout does not "see" anything but the recognition point? That is, the entirety of the fly means little or nothing to the trout if the recognition point is based on colour. To put the supposition clearer, perhaps trout take a fly because a portion of that fly is attractive to them and the greater success of some flies is because they incorporate a whole host of recognition points sometimes of different natural creatures. This would explain why various people can visualise different aquatic creatures in the same pattern of fly.

Remember that, in this section, we are isolating colour importance as opposed to form importance and movement importance. In practice, a good working fly should incorporate recognition points of all three but, for the moment, back to colour.

I have had an experiment going for a while now which although based on conjecture (as are many other flyfishing theories) seems to suggest that there may be some substance to the idea formulated above.

The fly has basic form and is composed of materials that allow maximum movement, but its interesting component is its colour variation. "Malcolm's Joseph" is made up of seven subtle colour changes. The object was not to create a gaudy fly, indeed in the water it could be likened to Clarkes' "calculated suggestion". That is, it is a likeness of something, which even though it may not exist, nevertheless looks as though it should exist.

I would go that step further and say that the object of the pattern is to be a caricature of a number of different identifiable aquatic creatures. Obviously if it is accepted that trout can pick out a particular recognition point during different time periods, then the scope of Joseph should be greatly enhanced.

Thus, while overall, Joseph could perhaps be said to be imitative (lowly) of a sedge pupa (during which period it is indeed extremely successful), its importance as an experiment is in the seven segmented recognition colours.

I do not believe that sufficient experimentation has taken place with Joseph to arrive at any concrete conclusions. Whatever its secret it is supremely successful, but the principle behind it is of greater interest.

In conclusion, somewhere along the line we have become lax in assessing the importance of colour. The chalkstream dry fly and nymph masters, whose ethics restricted their use of movement, laid great emphasis on subtlety of colour. We should perhaps not dismiss it lightly.

2. THE IMPORTANCE OF MOVEMENT

In assessing movement, we should clarify what we mean by movement. For now we will concentrate on the manner in which the fly is tied, rather than movement created solely by a retrieve. In other words, a brick drawn through the water has movement of an external nature, but none of an inbuilt quality.

There is no doubt that the ability of a fly to suggest life is literally half the battle won. Many "perfect imitations" fall down in this category, because the endeavour to reproduce a carbon copy in the vice, in many cases, sacrifices those materials which can flutter and wriggle.

As with colour, there is a subtlety involved which can induce a trout to "take". An incident which occurred at the English water, Damerham, serves as an excellent example. In the calm, clear water, I had spotted a quartet of rainbows browsing quietly along, some fifteen metres out. I put a fly out and in the windless water, I could see every movement of the fish. The heaviest of the group, obviously interested, but wary, edged along behind the fly which I tweaked in. It was really quite frustrating for I had the distinct feeling that the trout was not convinced by the fly's performance. Every time the fly moved forward an inch, so did the trout. When the fly stopped, the trout followed suit. Just then a friendly squall of wind ruffled the surface of the water. I stopped retrieving to allow the squall to pass over the area of the fly. In that instant, I could not see the artificial clearly, but instantaneously, the trout smashed into it. It was quite clear that the wind movement, delicate as it had been, was the inducement that the trout had been waiting for.

A little exercise I have since endeavoured to carry out, is to drop the fly I have just tied on into the water and observe its in-built movement as it sinks. In this way, one can be sure that even when the fly is not being retrieved, it is not a completely dead object.

Movement, whether internal or external, was earlier defined as suggestion — likeness in movement. Although neither Halford nor Skues would have relied to any extent on external movement, later writers have pinpointed its efficiency. Indeed, Sawyer's tactic of simply raising the rod at the appropriate moment was sufficient to give birth to "the Netheravon style" and the "induced take". Kite was even more emphatic and stressed the employment of the artificial in a lifelike manner.

The chalkstream writers obviously made use of the river currents to give the fly movement where nymph was used, but naturally enough, stillwater anglers had no such natural assistance. With the increasing popularity of imitative patterns in stillwater patterns, there was a move to study the natural movement of the aquatic creatures in order to improve the suggestive qualities of the fly.

Again, in accordance with the caricature approach, it wasn't long before it was argued that exaggerated movement had its advantages. One should be careful not simply to confuse exaggerated movement with retrieving the fly faster, where one might induce an aggressive reaction.

I believe that with the accent on "lure" fishing, we are all a little guilty of fishing too quickly and perhaps, in addition, not paying sufficient attention to the movement created by virtue of the in-built characteristics of the fly. After all, few aquatic creatures have been known to swim as quickly, or as long, as most of the flies that are retrieved — even allowing for exaggerated movement.

External movement created by a retrieve is sadly a neglected part of the flyfisher's armoury. The supposed anomaly in the statement "I was fishing the same fly as he was, but he caught all the fish" is often explained when one watches the attention paid to the retrieve. Knowing what fly to use is one thing; knowing how to use it, is another.

3. THE IMPORTANCE OF FORM

Amongst imitative anglers the importance of form, or relative proportion is stressed. Yet, while the caricature followers do not espouse such preciseness, their adherence to exaggeration of characteristics, by definition, must include an appreciation of form. Two examples of where form is adhered to, is in the simulation of the dragonfly and damselfly nymph patterns.

Form most commonly refers to shape, but an offshoot of this which has caused a great deal of comment, is the part played by size. Halford mentioned it and Skues, somewhat surprisingly in his earlier writings excluded form as a prerequisite to success, but agreed that size was paramount. Later he suggested that stomach content analysis should include an examination of form and that nymph representations should match dimensions, outline and proportion. Whether he meant that such adherence was necessary for the catching of fish is not that clear, for the reason, given by Skues was that, if these particulars were not contemplated, it would "discredit the true art of nymph fishing and lend a handle to these dry fly fanatics who want to put back the clock and re-establish the rigid and exclusive despotism of the dry fly." One senses, by the way, a frustration in Skues, for he dedicated his earlier "Minor Tactics of the Chalk Stream" to " . . . my friend the dry fly purist".

Ogden in 1879, placed size alongside colour as crucial, but latterly, little emphasis seems to have been placed on size of fly. Certainly the average South African angler doesn't worry himself too much about changing the size of the fly as opposed to the pattern. If a size 8 Connemara Black is unsuccessful, few would change to a size 14.

It is really only when one does stomach contents analysis that one appreciates just how big our flies are in comparison to the majority of trouty delicacies.

4. THE IMPORTANCE OF TEXTURE

Richard Walker was one of the few anglers to draw attention to the importance of texture of the fly. What exactly he meant by this is open to interpretation, but I believe there is merit in the thought that the trout is more likely to reject an artificial comprising hard unyielding material than one made up of soft, yielding fibres (of course the softer materials are more able to create movement which in itself is an inducement to tie such flies).

In our South African conditions, one does not readily have opportunities to assess the true rejection rate, but I can say this. In any fishing day, it is quite probable, particularly if a sinking line is being used, that unbeknown to us, our flies are sampled and rejected by fish. Indeed, if we did not actively "tighten up" on trout, they would, in most cases, ultimately expel the fly.

The delicacy with which a trout can sample a fly has to be seen to be believed — and sometimes one cannot believe one's eyes. The most illuminating example I can give, occurred initially on New Zealand's Tongariro River. I was fishing the Jones pool in the conventional manner by casting a big Red Setter across to the opposite bank; allowing it to sink and ultimately to swing round in the current. However, instead of immediately retrieving, I would hold the rod out towards the middle of the river and allow the fly to "swim" in the flow for a few seconds. If nothing happened, I would then begin the retrieve.

During the period in which I allowed the fly to swim, I held the line to feel for a "take" and, into the bargain, watched my rod tip. After a few casts, I became aware that, seemingly with the changing flow of the current, my rod tip would drift forward a few inches and then back again. This happened twice and although I could feel nothing, I wondered whether the movement was as innocent as it appeared. The next time it happened I did something I seldom do — I struck. The result: a 5 lb angry fresh run rainbow hen. This observation brought me a number of good fish and two years later, on the Waitahanui I took an 8 lb 10 oz cock in identical fashion.

I have a feeling that these fish were simply inhaling the fly and then expelling it; a procedure I watched with interest some years previously at Avington in England. At no stage in any of the abovementioned cases did I actually feel anything.

Any flyfisher who uses a floating line regularly will testify to the fact that he is able to see many takes long before he feels any resistance. I have had occasion to tutor a number of anglers in the use of floating line tactics over the past year and have constantly been amazed at the number of takes which they do not register and which do not result in hooked fish. Although such delicate opportunities can take place at any time, one of the common periods is as the fly (usually a leaded pattern) is sinking. If one is watching the leader which sinks progressively, it is quite common to see the nylon suddenly accelerate its sinking rate, for six inches or so. If the angler does not react by tightening up, the trout in nine out of ten occasions will reject the fly and the unconcerned flyfisher will be blissfully unaware. In stillwater angling this is not an easy exercise to follow. The concentration level has to be extremely high and is tiring. If windy conditions prevail it can be nigh on impossible.

At Dullstroom Dam not long ago, I ended up with a good bag while my three compatriots were fishless. We attributed it entirely to the fact that I had picked up the soft takes and reacted.

I could go on with further examples, but I believe the point has been made and I know most experienced anglers have had similar encounters.

CONCLUSION

In discussing the importance of colour, movement, form and texture I come to the realisation that the South African angler is, in the main, not terribly concerned with expecting as much of his fly as he is entitled to. Commercial fly tyers do a good job in filling an obvious need and they cannot really be expected to meet such exacting requirements without a commensurate increase in price. Commercial flies do catch fish and it may well be argued that to wish for more out of a pattern is merely academic.

Without doubt a good fly, which has the right qualities, is a tremendous psychological and practical advantage. As mentioned previously, materials substitution in the tying of flies has taken place over the years and, in many cases, this substitution has not occurred as a result of scarcity, but rather to improve speed of turnover and cost saving. Inevitably the qualities which "make" a fly are eroded and its performance is not up to the standard which its originator demanded.

This is not a criticism of commercially tied flies. They do the job they are intended to do. At the same time there is plenty of scope for the amateur fly tyer to concentrate on.

CHAPTER 8

Dabbling on the Fly Tying Front

SOME LIGHT-HEARTED ENCOUNTERS

For someone who aspires to having a streak of creativity running through him, my earliest attempts at fly tying were distinctly uninspiring. Even the first half-pounder that ripped my flimsily-tied Red Devil apart, probably only did so after the manner of a teacher tearing up a worthless composition.

Then came a host of other apparitions bearing titles such as Brut (Big Red Ugly Thing), Mad Coachman, Sparrman Special, Red Molo, Riki-Tiki Muddler and Bally Mally. They all caught fish, but with the exception of the Red Molo, they had nothing to commend them.

Even the Red Molo (which was closely followed by the Green Molo and Black Molo) was not as important in character as it was in principle. Kite may have had his bare-hook nymph; I had my Molo patterns.

What they did however, was to form a basis for some of my theories on imitation and caricature. And, even allowing for my own inadequacies in fly tying, I never again worried about trying to copy anything in an exact fashion.

MORE SERIOUS EXPERIMENTS

Out of the early conglomeration, some patterns of note appeared. With an aroused interest in entomology and an absorption with theoretical aspects, these creations were developed perhaps with more thought and purpose.

1. BOURKE'S LUCK

The first to establish itself was Bourke's Luck. A fry imitation, it came about in June 1975 as an aid to some work I was putting in on theories of aggression in trout. A secondary aspect was the omission of the colour red. A common ground rule, at the time, in the Eastern Transvaal, was that a fly, to have success, had to have some red in it.

A second point to note is that the final characteristics of the fly did not come in one inspired flash of brilliance. The artificial I called Bourke's Luck underwent sometimes drastic changes in its formative years. Its attachment to an unconventional wide gape silver hook gave it an unusual action and shape in the water.

Today it's a conventional pattern, conventionally tied and I feel a bit sad that its rebellious fire has settled down to middle-aged smouldering.

It was, and is, supremely successful and at one stage had an ability to take big fish (relatively speaking) out of the most unlikely places. Within a month it had a 4 lb 2 oz fish out of one of the Oshoek dams (⅛ acre) and then one hot mid-morning in October while I was waiting to speak to the late Dolf Combrink, owner of Elandskloof, I put Bourke's Luck into the caravan park dam (No. 16) and amongst hordes of kids, Uncles and Aunties pulled out a cockfish of 4½ lbs. Now I have fished that dam for years and never caught anything over 1½ lbs.

2. TADPOLE

The second fly of interest to emanate was the Tadpole fly. It all really started during a week-end's fishing with John Goddard, world famous angler-entomologist, John Ketley (later to be England flyfishing captain), Trevor Babich and myself. I remember John Goddard being enthralled at the size of our flying ants and John Ketley trying to emulate the tadpole's tail with a cock hackle. That was it! A fly comprising one cock hackle — and it was successful. I simply worked from there.

The Tadpole, for a long time, was always good for one or two fish, but was not as prolific producer as Bourkes Luck. In addition it seemed to be more acceptable to Natal trout. I remember being quite pleased at getting a 3¾ lb rainbow from Riverside dam (N.F.F.C.) and then one day at Ron-Ann dam, another Club water, the trout went mad for it.

I believe that I don't use this pattern as much as I should. Like many of the New Zealand flies, the tail tends to wrap around the hook, which can be frustrating, but to shorten the tail is to destroy that superb action it has.

3. KERING'ENDE NYMPH

Most fly tyers have at some stage attempted to tie a dragonfly nymph imitation, and the Kering'ende nymph was no exception. It was tied with materials which did not allow for a great amount of movement, but was leaded with the foil from an old wine bottle.

Its début was at the popular Eastern Transvaal resort, Elandskloof. I tackled up one lovely May day at the biggest dam (No. 13) intending to fish one of my favourite channels. It's the sort of spot, where, if you can manage to fish it before anybody else, you're almost guaranteed a trout or two.

The channel runs reasonably deep, so I attached the "new boy" to a sinking line and put out a long cast. Because the fly was leaded, I began retrieving immediately, albeit extremely slowly. There would be a stuttering sort of take and then a strong pull. Twenty minutes of fishing produced four good fish for the water.

It was only then that I discovered that the fly had been acceptable to the trout even though as a result of the lead foil it had been swimming upside down!

4. ABERDARE NYMPH

Fluorescent materials have been in vogue for some time and certainly overseas they are popular. New Zealand in 1985 was inundated with yellow, orange, red and multi-mixed glo-bug yarn creations, which were on the brink of being banned. And any reader of English trout fishing magazines will have had his eyes assailed by garish monstrosities, which would look more at home punctured through the lobe of a punk rocker's ear.

In 1980 I had, on the banks of England's Packington fishery, swapped flies with the local brethren. One of the nymph patterns I acquired had a fluorescent green backside and this little neon light attracted trout most successfully.

On my return to South Africa I experimented with a half-thought lure called Piskie Green, which fell into the category: When all else fails, try this.

I suppose under the conditions it performed well, picking up the odd trout around dusk (it really was a last cast effort) but I thought: if the fluorescence was incorporated into a calculated suggestion nymph, it could have merit, particularly in weather conditions of half-light.

The little fellow thus born was the Aberdare nymph. Its first outing was in mid-winter on a sombre July morning. Some weeks previously on a pre-dawn patrol on the same Eastern Transvaal dam, I had taken a 6 lb fish in excellent conditions and hopes were high for another good fish.

The Aberdare nymph with its dimly glowing thorax searched around for a while and then settled for a hen of 6 lb 2 oz.

This artificial is a perfect example of a fly blossoming under certain light conditions. Because of the fluorescence it stands out, but the same occurs with many normal flies. Some days, a particular pattern will seem to have a visibility that makes it most attractive; on other days it is but a drab shadow.

5. PLEWMAN'S KILLER

For some years I had noticed trout in our Eastern Transvaal dams feeding heavily on midge larva. It struck me as distinctly odd that nymph patterns should be so widespread and yet larva patterns were all but unknown. It was not as though anglers were unaware of the incidence of larva in stomach contents, but even here, this knowledge was more confined to the easily recognisable bloodworm.

Olive midge larva far outnumbered the bloodworm and it seemed reasonable to suppose that a pattern along these lines would do well. The difficulty is that the olive larvae do not appear to lend themselves to the caricature approach. They are small and worm-like and so was the fly I developed. The olive hue was not difficult to match and the wriggling motion was settled with a few strands of marabou. Larvae have a sheen to their appearance and I tied in two strands of flashabou along the length of the fly.

It worked, but when I added a seemingly insignificant touch of scarlet silk just behind the head it improved dramatically. On a "hard" week-end at Middelpunt, on an intermediate line, it picked up half-a-dozen trout where none were previously to be had.

My Dad was seriously ill in hospital and I desperately wanted a fly for him. One visiting time, I took the fly in and asked him to name it.

Dad's no longer with us, but Plewman's Killer is.

6. DIGGERS RED

If an olive midge larva pattern is worth recreating, then certainly so is the bloodworm. One would think that the tying should be the same as for the olive midge larva, but for a substitution in colour. Yet Diggers Red is differently tied and don't ask me why. Somehow it looks better! (If you think women are fickle, just watch a fly tyer in action!)

I confess I haven't taken any big bags yet, but I believe it's only a matter of time.

7. MALCOLM'S JOSEPH

Like Bourke's Luck, this pattern originated out of a desire to experiment.

We have mentioned Joseph before and the principle behind it, but if I did not take it too seriously at the time of first tying, I certainly do now. From the first moment I started fishing it, it caught fish, in circumstances, I might add, where trout were few and far between. Nevertheless, I only really pricked up my ears when other anglers started echoing my experiences.

It is a prolific fish catcher and while it is still too early to judge the principle upon which it is based, I expect great things in the future.

Normally I dislike self-named flies, but in the manner of Turnbull-Kemp's "Water Mongoose" which others insisted on referring to as Kemp's Favourite, so too has the original name been thrust aside by opinion.

CHAPTER 9

Choice of Fly

Thus far we have examined the various characteristics of flies and their imitative and/or suggestive roles. In theory therefore, we should have a much better idea of those flies which are more likely to produce results when the fish are feeding on one or more aquatic creatures.

The practical problem is to ascertain, prior to the capture of a fish, which aquatic creatures are in vogue. There are a number of ways to do this; some rather more involved than others, but remember we will be extremely fortunate to come up with the right answer immediately. Most anglers follow one of three approaches. Either they:
(1) revert to a favourite or general all-round fly
(2) they refer to past experience, or
(3) they begin angling only once they have, on current observation, concocted a logical basis for selection.

There is a fourth method. It's called: shake your hat and see which fly falls out.

1. THE FAVOURITE FLY SYNDROME

This is a very common approach and, I might add, an extremely successful one. So many angling writers have alluded to the power of confidence, that it must not be underestimated. Confidence in a fly makes one concentrate harder and fish more intelligently. Even Halford whose code of ethics totally forbade choice of fly based on favouritism, admitted that if an angler had such confidence in a fly, he should not exclude it.

Some flyfishers have favourites to the exclusion of all others but I believe, with experience, the absolute faith in a fly is reduced to the concept of what I might call "a fly for all seasons". In other words, the experienced angler who is not employing methods (2) or (3) will build up a shortlist of all-round flies which he can rely on to produce results on most occasions. At this stage it may be wondered why the angler does not simply limit himself to these patterns, if they are so reliable. I can only answer for myself. Apart from all other enjoyable aspects of flyfishing, one of the challenges is often not simply to catch a fish, but to catch it in a certain fashion. Reliability does not mean the best fly in particular circumstances.

These all-round general patterns do change through the years, but I have four at the moment: Walkers Killer, Peacock Woolly Worm, Joseph and Muddler Minnow.

As I said earlier, these flies are usually good enough, in the absence of further information, to winkle out a trout or two. Once a trout has been taken, the information gained thereby can lead one to prefer some other avenue.

2. PAST EXPERIENCE

I don't suppose there are too many anglers who adopt the Victorian habit of keeping a diary, but I confess, even though I believe I have an excellent memory, there is no chance that I could remember anything but the more memorable.

The problem is that the more memorable is usually so, because it is unusual and therefore we tend to mentally record the exception to the rule. The common occurrences can somehow pass us by. I have kept certain information since I caught my first trout and that basic information has been a gold mine with which to form a basis of opinion.

In the context of flies I have tried to maintain two lines of thought. These are successful patterns used and stomach contents analysed.

When, however, one matches these findings from year to year, patterns do emerge that are usually quite accurate and from which one can benefit. With respect to stomach contents analysis, some findings are general and are in vogue all year round, while others are seasonal to a degree. Depending on weather conditions, the appearance of aquatic creatures can be hastened or delayed, but they are nevertheless expected. Two overseas examples of some fame come immediately to mind. These relate to the Mayfly hatches in the UK, and in New Zealand the "smelting" period beginning around October.

With particular relevance to the Transvaal and Natal stillwaters I have found the following guidelines to be most useful, although they are not exact, nor by any means exhaustive. While other aquatic creatures may also attract the trout's attention, particular emphasis should be placed on exploiting these feeding preferences.

A. SEPTEMBER TO APRIL — DAPHNIA

I have deliberately refrained from placing any emphasis on the aggressive instinct of the trout which can be exploited by the use of fast moving lure. However, there are, as I see it, two situations which in the context of this book, deserve mention, although it may be difficult to separate the part played by aggression as opposed to the feeding motive.

"Trout on the Veld" goes into detail on aggressive theories and also the trout's preoccupation with the minute water flea, daphnia. It thus serves little purpose to repeat those pages except to say that as the water warms up, so the daphnia blooms become more active. When daphnia are deep, the importance of colour in the fly diminishes, but a real giveaway is the appearance of algae floating under the surface. In such conditions, usually muggy, hot weather, daphnia will be found closer to the surface and should the angler be within range, an orange fly such as the Red Setter, is a good bet. And it's not essential that it be a big pattern, nor that it be moved fast either.

While the daphnia usually is of a rust colour (not terribly apparent to the naked eye) I have come across, in exceptional circumstances, a daphnia of a greenish hue. This has only occurred early in the season.

B. SEPTEMBER TO MAY — SNAIL

A favoured trout delicacy, there is still much confusion as to how this feeding can be exploited. One must, I believe, try and distinguish whether the trout are picking snail up from bottom weed and mud, or whether they are taking floating snail off the surface. From stomach contents this can sometimes be ascertained as the trout's intake includes bits of such detritus as well. On the other hand, a slow deliberate, perhaps even head-and-tail rise in the early morning may indicate that the fish are feeding on snail in the surface film. (This particular rise form is not exclusive to snail however).

As bourgeois as it may appear, I've often found that a small fat Walkers Killer (size 10-12), moved slowly along the bottom has taken its fair share of snail feeding rainbows, but I've no doubt that the Coch-y-bonddhu would do equally well as would a Coachman.

Where the snail is on the surface, the same patterns would be effective, but I rather like my Irresistibles (14's) providing that they are fished in the surface film and not as a conventional dry fly. This means one has to give them a bit of a soaking and not too much false casting. (One can use a felt tipped pen to darken the deer hair body, if need be.)

The point to make is that once a cast is made and the fly settled in the surface film, resist the temptation to retrieve. By all means take up slack, but don't be impatient. The trout knows his quarry is not going away and he's really in no hurry.

(Contrast this with a similar tactic used on sedge feeding trout).

One further point to make is that as the floating snail has no mobility of its own, it will be at the mercy of the wind. If there is a breeze, watch the ripple line carefully; the snail will all be in that line and it is not uncommon to see one or more fish on patrol picking them off.

C. AUGUST TO DECEMBER — TADPOLES

When reaching the waterside, never neglect to observe those creatures inhabiting the shallows. Sometimes there are corixa scuttling away, other times pin head fry, but it may just be that, collected in droves, are small black tadpoles, which are made up simply of a blob and wriggly tail.

Because they tend to remain in the shallows, often no more than a foot or two off the side, the trout have to take chances to get to them and so I would, upon spotting the tadpoles, recommend an early morning sortie with a small Taddy or even a Kenya Bug which can be deadly.

Of tadpoles and frogs there are certain strategic offshoots that do occur, but before we go into that, depending on when the actual annual breeding takes place, it is likely that some of the platanna tadpoles (as opposed to Rana) will be large enough to make a mouthful. A big Tadpole fly will bring dividends.

Each year I watch for the time when the frogs begin to get active, knowing that if the nuptials are soon to begin, the offspring will not be far behind.

Because of the frenetic activity which can be observed by countless miniature rises, the bigger trout are often attracted and it is at these times that one will find adult frogs in stomach contents.

The irritating thing about this particular period is that the frogs too are very aggressive and will take a slow moving fly readily. Nymph fishing can become a joke.

D. FEBRUARY TO MAY — SEDGE

One of the scenes that stirs my imagination is the sight of that ungainly "moth" fluttering unsteadily along between the marginal reeds. My immediate thought is that there are sedge around and because of the speed with which the pupa hatches into the adult sedge, the simple fact of sedge bumbling around means that the fish will not only be vulnerable to the dry fly, but also to a thoughtfully fished pupal pattern.

Sedge can appear from nowhere. One minute the day is empty; the next there's a dozen fluttering around. One time at Sterkfontein Dam I had waded out and in the ripple observed the odd fish splashing. I watched the water carefully and, in front of my eyes, an adult sedge appeared as if by magic. I had to shake my head a bit, for I had indeed observed in the disturbed water, a pupa which had come up from the bottom and hatched as it hit the surface.

I will be mentioning dry fly methods but, suffice to say, when one sees those splashy excited rises, a small Irresistible or Sedge pattern will inspire some great fishing. And watch the trout's actions closely. If your dry fly is getting a lot of short takes, dump it in the surface film, or even better, after a short rise, leave the fly there and wait for the action to begin.

Sedge hatches can be sporadic. I've not really known them to be continuous, but they can be episodical. There'll be tremendous activity for a quarter of an hour, then it will slowly die down. Just as suddenly, twenty minutes later the second act will begin. And so it goes on.

Just the fact that I know sedge have hatched at some stage is enough for me to try larva and pupal imitations. I have tried most of the recommended patterns such as Invicta and have had success but, biased as I am, I have unshakeable confidence in Joseph. Fished on a floating line I have found a size 8 to be most productive when there is not that much activity going on, but when the fish begin to rise and I have not yet switched to dry fly, a size 12 Joseph can reap rewards.

Although I have earmarked sedge for consideration during the February-May period, with the exception of the coldest months, I have come across them throughout the year.

E. MARCH TO JULY — FRY

Beginning in autumn, it is not unusual to find small fry scuttling around the shoals. Perhaps it's a bad time to be a Barbus minnow particularly in Natal, because apart from the cooler water inducing the larger trout to stay longer in the margins, those larger trout are feeling the first stirrings of their spawning urges — an urge which can further inflame the aggressive instincts of the trout, particularly if they happen upon a shoal of the little fellows who, in response, will set up a massive panic reaction.

Once again, even if it is a chilly morning, dawn patrol will often uncover these trout hunting the shallows. In water deep enough to a broad flank, these big fish will take fry readily.

I suppose any fry imitator is useful in such circumstances, because the trout's feeding instincts are reinforced by aggression. Thus, any lure setting up the right type of vibration will be effective.

However, I like the Muddler option, especially later in the morning when there is not quite so much activity going on. Using a sinking line and the conventional Muddler (the sparse chap with a turkey wing) one can emulate a small wounded Minnow quite remarkably. Fish it around weedbeds, structure or even in shallow bays and any prospective foragers will find it difficult not to be tempted.

At such times of the year, a fish caught will regurgitate its previous victim and the condition of such prey leads me to believe that if a big Muddler is being used, ie, size 4-8, the chances are that the first "take" will be more of a knock. Try not to react until a firm pull is felt; it may be that the first assault is just to stun the prey.

Indeed a friend and I, not long ago, at a N.F.F.C. dam in May had a succession of lost fish. My recollection is that they were cockfish and had been skimpily hooked around the snout.

F. APRIL TO AUGUST — TERRESTRIALS

Terrestrials are naturally enough around most of the time, but it would seem as though the trout cotton on to them during these months with particular relish. It may be that the trout are feeding on everything they can prior to spawning, or it may simply be that, as the veld thins out and fires are to be commonly observed, that terrestrials are more vulnerable particularly in a strong wind.

Under "terrestrials" is a conglomeration of crawling, flying, hopping things, from ladybirds, beetles, bumble bees, caterpillars and last, but not least, grasshoppers (and the odd daddy-long-legs).

There's not that much to go on, except the daddy's which, in my experience thus far, are infrequent, and the grasshoppers. The last time I looked, the trout at the Invicta Club waters, had gorged themselves on a multitude of green and red hoppers which went by various disgusting names.

The method I like the most is not dissimilar to one mentioned earlier which inspanned the use of the Muddler Minnow. In this case, while the conventional Muddler will work satisfactorily, there is a variation which does incorporate green and red and, which, one might suggest, goes that step further.

A sinking line can be used if one wishes to mix Muddler tactics up, ie. fish "grasshopper" on the surface and, when retrieving, "minnow" on the bottom, but if they are taking hoppers on the surface, a floater is a better option.

I've found the rise to the fly to be confusing, so I watch the Muddler like a hawk and if there is any disturbance near the fly I begin a slow retrieve until the pull is felt. Something (or nothing) will happen after about three pulls. Once again I fish the fly motionless and even if there is a wind I like to put the fly into a patch of calm water, if at all possible.

G. CAENIS — SEPTEMBER TO APRIL

During the hotter months, a fairly common host will welcome you to the waterside on a balmy still evening. Extremely gregarious he is and although minute, is hard to miss. Rising in white columns he will attach himself to your person and even make use of the opportunity to transform his being from dun to spinner, leaving behind the telltale white shucks.

Trout feed avidly on the nymph of the caenis through to the spent spinner stage and even the shucks are sometimes found in stomach contents. Whether the fish have taken the shucks by mistake or whether they have sampled the rapidly emerging adult is not clear.

Imitative angling during a caenis hatch is difficult, particularly when the spent spinners lie with wings outstretched in the surface film. However, I have found that, prior to this, trout will feed avidly on the nymph and this opens up an avenue of attack. I ignore the trout that may be feeding on the surface (which is not easy) and fish with a small imitation (10-14) or Walkers yellow nymph. My quarry are lower down in the water and so although there is plenty of competition around, the trout are at least aware of my fly. Trout feeding on the spent spinner are so close to the surface that the problem is that unless you are able to put the fly on his nose, he is not even aware of the artificial.

Fishing during such periods, although not easy, is usually overstated in terms of despondence. We have been conditioned to the basic misconception that because the fish are feeding avidly, they should be easier to catch. The duration of a caenis hatch can vary, but in general the angler in summer will spend between 1-2 hours being taunted. How many 1-2 hour periods during the day do we spend, getting not a touch, yet not considering it "hard" fishing. Yet in the caenis cocktail hour, if we only get one fish, we are not impressed. Trout, unbeknown to us, refuse our offerings time and time again when we fish sub-surface, thus it should come as no surprise that they will do so, when they are on the surface. A small deerhair imitation or Muddler Minnow can induce a take, but I've found it is of more consequence to concentrate on extreme accuracy and a quick casting technique.

H. DRAGONFLY AND DAMSELFLY NYMPHS

Of all the aquatic creatures, the dragonfly and damselfy nymphs lend themselves to imitation and South African flyfishers have had a good go at stretching their imaginations on the vice. I like to have a few suitable patterns at all times in my flybox as, where there is a weedbed, there are usually natural nymphs around. However, towards the back end of the season, the dragonfly nymphs certainly come into their own and stomach contents can yield some absolute monsters. The damselfly nymphs seem to be more apparent in summer. One further method is to observe whether adult dragonflies or damselflies are around.

The Natal boys have some really good imitations of both, but one of the most effective dragon patterns is, believe it or not, the Mrs Simpson, Walkers Killer (tied Mrs Simpson-style) and the Hamills Killer.

As far as the damselfly nymph is concerned, if you haven't got any of the tuf-chenille creations made up, improvisation can take place with a Muddler (small size) or Sawyer's pheasant tail nymph (large sizes).

The standard floating line procedures fished over and around weedbeds are the most successful.

I. MIDGE LARVAE AND PUPAE

Another standard all-round consideration concerns exploiting the midge population. As far as the pupa is concerned, warm summer evenings are times to be aware of and although buzzer imitations are on sale in the tackle shops, small Connemara Blacks, Black Gnats and even the Coachman (later on in the evening) can be brought into play.

Midge pupa hatches are obviously not restricted to evenings and can occur at any time, even sometimes at midday, but one indication is the head-and-tailing trout. (Don't automatically assume that it is midge pupa that are present, but it does cut down the options).

The other interesting aspect is that midge pupae can be fished at various levels, but they are at their most vulnerable when trapped suspended in the surface film. Some anglers try and keep their imitations at surface level by greasing the leader and others use variations of John Goddard's suspender midge.

I have alluded to the preponderance of larvae around throughout the year and the apparent lack of respect that anglers show them. The two colours that predominate the most are red and olive but I have for some time been watching the appearance of the phantom larva. The three flies I like the most are Diggers Red, Plewman's Killer and as far as the phantom larva is concerned, the Baby Doll. In its Dr Jeckyl role, Malcolm's Joseph is a good all-round larva imitation.

J. SEASONAL ROUND-UP

I have hopefully given some idea of the times when one can expect certain things to happen in the aquatic world. If one is on the lookout for these occasions, a lot of satisfaction can be had.

By using past experiences, one can almost anticipate sedge or minnow fishing and be prepared for such in advance.

There are many more mini-circumstances that can rear their heads. Flying ants, corixa, leeches and a number more can suddenly pop up and test your skill. Noting these in your diary can one day add up to a pattern.

3. OBSERVING THE CURRENT SITUATION — BE OBSERVANT

If an angler knows he has flies in his armoury that he can rely on and he has a pretty reasonable idea of what might await him, it's more than likely that he will start off the day with confidence. However, his determination of the fly (or more precisely, flies) on the day, will come about through an observation of his surroundings.

This observation process should continue throughout the day, for conditions will change and the sooner the angler is aware of this, the sooner he will be able to take advantage of it.

Strangely enough, the strength of the "all flies are equal" proposition comes about when anglers congregate at the end of the day and compare successful flies. Should there be a diversity of patterns, the conclusion is often reached that choice of fly had to be unimportant. Yet the alternative possibility is that the trout were caught at different times of the day, with different tactics and in different places and therefore it is more probable that specific conditions prevailing dictated the use of alternatives.

— WHAT NATURAL FLY OR AQUATIC CREATURES ARE PRESENT

We have already alluded to one area in which one should increase awareness and that is to be on the lookout for various aquatic creatures. Tadpoles and fry in the shallows; sedge fluttering amongst the reeds; dragonfly and damselfly darting hither and thither. These are all excellent indications upon which to base a selection.

— WATER AND LIGHT CONDITIONS

Another indicator is the clarity of the water. Perhaps I do also suffer at times from the phobia: If I can't see my fly, then neither can the trout. If the water is murky, or discoloured, I tend to use bigger patterns with a well-defined outline. These patterns such as the Woolly Worm or "killer" series, although dark in colour do stand out better in murky water. To some extent, the same occurs in light conditions where the water appears dark yet nevertheless is clear. This is usually in a flat calm where the water has, what I call, a "dead" character about it. It looks lifeless too. To offset the lack of movement which wave action can impart, I like the selected pattern to have a lot of in-built movement.

This brings me to an interesting point and one which I find difficult in explaining. Light conditions play a part in determining the "colour" of the water. Taken in conjunction with the physical attributes of the water eg. peat, weed bottom, gravel bottom, etc. this "colour" has an effect on the fly. The only way I determine this phenomenon is to sink the fly in the water and observe its overall visibility. Sometimes a fly stands out; it looks good. Other times it just doesn't exude the same vibrancy. In clear water, whether it be at dawn or dusk, I find that the use of flies which have fluorescent materials, eg. Aberdare nymph, do well.

Thus, although it sounds as though I am advocating a "Bright day bright fly, etc." theory it is not quite so simple. Unless I am pretty certain about my selection of a pattern, I place great emphasis on this visibility. I think this is why some flies do well in certain dams and in certain areas.

In extremely clear water it is more than likely that I would prefer smaller flies and those which are of sparser dressing.

— FISH MOVEMENTS

The observation of fish movements is one which usually makes the heart of any angler happy, yet if proper observation is not carried out it can turn into a most frustrating experience. The first distinction to be made is whether the fish moving is feeding or not and it is usually not difficult to tell. A fast moving fish is one that apparently has more on its mind than food and it is not uncommon to see the same fish moving repeatedly along a certain beat.

These fish don't seem to be too perturbed about anglers and apart from increasing their rate of swimming, they seem to lack the fear that they would normally exhibit at other times. The other non-feeding movements that commonly are observed are at spawning time when there is much ado in the shallows, or the laboured swimming of a sick fish.

But back to feeding movements. We have already mentioned some, eg. fry feeders and head-and-tailers and the principle is therein incorporated. A "rise" is not just a rise, but an indicator of that which the trout is feeding on and the level at which the fish is positioned.

For example, a common enough statement is that a head-and-tailing trout is usually feeding on midge pupa or floating snail. I would not argue with this except to say, that it is more the characteristics of the food form which induce such behaviour than the mere aquatic creature itself. This stems from my observations of head-and-tailers at times when the trout were patently neither feeding on midge pupa nor snail. The common denominator however was that the foodsort was lying just under the surface film and was helpless — and the trout knew it.

Head-and-tailing is essentially a smooth, unhurried activity and as long as the trout is convinced that his prey is at his mercy, he is not going to expend any unnecessary energy.

Thus, the important aspects as far as I am concerned, are in realising that head-and-tailing trout indicate surface film food which is not going anywhere fast.

Whereas a head-and-tailer has to be visually observed (because it is so quiet) a splashy rise can be heard from some distance away. The first assumption is that whatever is keeping the trout busy is on top of the water, ie. an adult fly and indeed one can listen for a "bloop" or see a resultant bubble which will confirm the surface activity. In short, you are being told to consider dry fly fishing as opposed to nymph fishing. The problem is to work out what adult fly is preoccupying the trout.

In the case of sedge, the rise is likely to be quite aggressive. In some cases, a lunge; in other cases a shower of spray. The adult sedge with its erratic flight is not easy to take off the surface and the trout will attempt to waterlog the insect's wings first and then to nail it as it flutters on the surface.

Once again, I believe the principle is more important and the trout will react in similar fashion to other creatures which behave as unpredictably as the sedge, eg. flying ants. I have seen trout following a sedge that has been fluttering along six inches above the surface; missing out on the splashing technique and then incredibly lunging out with head and shoulders to take the sedge in mid-flight.

The third important visual movement to identify is the boil at the surface, which can mislead anglers to believe that a fish has risen. There is usually quite a substantial movement of water, but the whole activity is silent, thus giving the clue that the fish has not been near the surface, but is probably feeding some feet down.

The fish could be feeding on a multitude of organisms and I would probably have to link this behaviour to other observations or past experience to arrive at the right answer. First and foremost however, is to gain an idea of the depth at which the fish is feeding and present the fly at that level.

There are other rise forms which go by various exotic names, but in all cases, one can establish a level of feeding which is important; in some cases a clue to the specific foodsort and if not, at least an approximation of how the food item is behaving.

CHAPTER 10

Some Ideas on Presentation

To date I have concentrated on the importance of the fly in trout fishing. We have largely ignored the part that aggression plays in the capture of trout and concentrated on the feeding habits of our South African fish. However, while it is obvious that I believe, on many occasions that choice of fly is important, it should go without saying that the various elements of presentation are just as critical.

Presentation, to my mind, has unfortunately been defined in a narrow sense and one gets the notion that it comprises the manner in which the trout sees the fly — almost synonymous with a good cast. If you land your fly on the water without too much disturbance, it's often said that that is a good presentation. And so it is, but it's not the whole story.

For instance, the method of moving the fly in the water — the retrieve — is also part of presentation. The means the angler uses to get his fly to the fish is another. And if one really follows this line of thought to its logical conclusion then the whole tactical process contributes to the art of presentation.

There are many ways to skin a cat and there are variations on variations. Most of these stem from basic strategies and it is upon these strategies that I would like to concentrate.

Flyfishing depends not only on knowing "how?" but also "why?" and it is always a combination that results in success.

1. PRACTICALLY SPEAKING

It's usual to find, through the passage of time, individual trout anglers having a preference for a certain mode of fishing. There is, of course, nothing wrong in this, just as there is nothing wrong in being a purist. There is so much to enjoy in flyfishing, that one should grant a fellow angler the right to choose his particular brand of enjoyment.

A priority in my life has been to travel widely and this I have achieved, with much of the travel amazingly coinciding with areas of the world in which trout are found. This penchant, both within and outside South Africa, has led me to numerous different venues, incorporating a wide variety of conditions. I have always regarded adaptability as being a prime requisite to successful flyfishing and, certainly if one is going to fish around, to limit one's outlook can hamper one to a great extent. Enjoyment comes in many forms and I have felt the same thrill battling out big rainbows in rushing rivers with a weight 9 lead-cored shooting head, as I have had taking three-quarter pound trout with a size 16 Irresistible on a weight 2 outfit. Not all of my friends accept such wide definition, but the important thing is that they respect my opinion as I respect theirs.

2. GENERAL OUTLOOK

I don't believe that the best way to learn the basics of any sport is through the pages of a book. Thus I would hesitate to go into reams on casting technique or the qualities of a rod, when even with a modicum of tuition, one can learn much more concerning the basics.

I have come to the conclusion that, in my present state of evolvement, I am happy with three different weight outfits. I have a weight 2, a weight 4/5 and an 8. What on earth, you may ask, does any angler want with such a diversity of tackle?

I used to think that big chaps used big rods; little fellows used little rods and that was that. Perhaps such was the case in the days of split cane, but with the advent of carbon fibre such distinctions need not be made.

When one finds a particular action in a rod to one's liking, it is really just a matter of adapting to the lighter weight rods. My reason for selecting the three outfits becomes a tactical and enjoyment decision. I feel that, being able to manipulate any of the outfits competently, means that there are few conditions that I cannot cope with. If there is a strong wind creating waves, I can take the big rod and still put out a reasonable line; if I am on a small heavily bushed stream, the delicacy of the 7 ft weight two combination, makes fishing a pleasure.

3. A DOLLY MIXTURE TO CHOOSE FROM
(a) FLOATERS

Over the past five years, a lot more anglers are to be found carrying along a floating line. "Carrying along" is the operative phrase, for this line is too seldom brought into use. The main reason for this reticence is that the idea persists that a floating line should be used exclusively for surface nymph and dry fly fishing. Thus, if the fish are not feeding in the top six inches of water, the floating line is not applicable.

Dispel that idea straight away. The floater is an extremely versatile piece of equipment that, with a bit of manipulation, allows us to fish the more productive depths in stillwater (4-10 ft down) with a great deal of sensitivity.

Another point to make is that the fly used need not be a dry fly nor a traditional-type nymph, but can be any size pattern of your choosing. One prerequisite to get the fly to sink, however, is to incorporate some lead into its make-up. Strangely enough, some moral distinction makes it permissible to wind lead wire around a fly, but not to use lead shot. (In England lead shot is banned by virtue of swans being poisoned). Since most commercially tied flies are not weighted, the lead shot approach may be considered, but I would recommend learning to tie your own flies, which you can then weight according to your preference. Weighting of a fly can also improve the action of the fly.

The second point is that the leader can be changed to assist in getting the fly down. Instead of the usual 9 ft leader one can extend to almost any length providing it is manageable. I usually find myself fluctuating between 12-18 ft.

We now have a leaded fly and a suitably lengthy leader. Unless conditions point to the contrary, I like to bring the fly in just over the bottom weed growth. Wait until the whole leader has sunk below the surface before retrieving. On a calm day, this will eliminate that herringbone wake, but in the main, by waiting, one minimises the bow between flyline and fly. This bow can cause one to lose direct touch with the fly and consequently the chance of missing a take is high.

The third element in the use of the floating line is concentration. One is no longer dependent on feeling the snatch of a taking trout, but the importance of visual angling becomes apparent. The majority of takes are seen before being felt — if one is observant. The appreciation of how many fish sample the fly becomes significantly more apparent.

(b) DOUBLING UP — THE USE OF DROPPERS

Neither the use of long leaders, nor the employment of a dropper is widespread in this country. One of the major reasons for this stems from the common use of the fast sinking line and there is no enjoyment emanating from continuously pulling weed free from two hooks. There are a multitude of other reasons usually advanced, varying from difficulty in casting, to losing fish on the encumbered hook which snags up.

I admit that there is some truth in these objections, but really not enough to gainsay the use of the dropper in certain circumstances. Some have commented that a dropper is unsporting, but this allegation can be summarily dismissed. One of the oldest traditional forms of stillwater flyfishing has for years, in the UK, meant the three fly approach, involving a bob fly, a dropper and a tail fly — commonly referred to as loch-style fishing.

The decision whether or not to use a dropper should revolve around risk. If one is not prepared to take the risk, then a dropper option should not be considered. Just for the record though, I have lost very few fish using this method and I cannot conclusively say, that it was the presence of the dropper that caused the loss on those occasions. The more immediate concern of the flyfisher is the instance where a second trout, attracted by the hooked fish, takes (usually the trailing tail fly).

The advantage of the dropper is not to try and hook two fish, but to open up more options in presentation. I do not use the dropper approach in conjunction with a sinking line, but confine it to the floater (or perhaps a sink-tip). Three major advantages come to mind, but I must caution that I would be wary of selecting a dropper in weedy water or one where a really big fish might be hooked.

The most common touted advantage is to give the fish a choice of patterns, especially if one is uncertain as to the feeding preference. For example, on a later summer's evening, the trout may be switching from sedge to midge pupa. The selection of appropriate patterns can save time and frustration.

Secondly, and aligned to the abovementioned, trout may be feeding at different levels and with the tail fly and dropper placed some feet apart, one can cut down on the uncertainty of not knowing where to present the fly especially at times of selectivity.

The third and essentially the most important reason to me, is the weight that the dropper gives in fishing with a floating line over the productive 4-10 ft water especially if one wishes to use small patterns.

Let's look at this a bit more carefully, as it is a bread-and-butter option. We wish to use a floating line and since we want to get a fly down, the leader needs some length to it. We are also of the opinion that the fish are taking small patterns. Such a pattern, even leaded within reason, will struggle on the long leader to get down to the desired depth. Ergo, the attachment of the dropper will assist. There is an alternative that might be considered — the intermediate or slow sinking line — but if one is fishing the small patterns slowly, these substitutes might not be able to keep the fly at the desired level for the length of the retrieve.

One observation I have made is that where the tail fly and the dropper are reasonably close together (±2 ft apart), my experience is that inevitably the tail fly is taken and the dropper's risk is thereby minimised.

The incidence of a 'double take' in South Africa is not that common, but I can say that this is an extremely productive method when used in the right circumstances.

(c) **TAKE ME TO YOUR LEADER**

There was a stage when my appreciation of the tactical use of the leader was pretty trite. The modus of flyfishing which I pursued and possibly the adherence to certain knots made it impractical and probably non-essential to strain my brain on this matter.

We have already, to a great extent, done away with some of the misconceptions concerning the use of the floating line. While fishing on or just below the surface, one can use any length of leader which gives one confidence or which aids visual presentation. Adapting the floating line to deeper fishing means lengthening the leader unless one is prepared to allow the floater to sink below the surface. The correct length will depend on your knowledge of the contours of the water, your summation of the situation and your ability to handle your tackle. I do not know of many anglers in South Africa who are happy to use leaders of 20 ft+, but it can be done with a bit of thought and appropriate conditions.

With a sinking line however, I would like to pass on some observations and experiences which I have had. In general, and with one exception, I do not favour a leader on a sinking line much in excess of 9 ft. In sinking line fishing, one imparts more action to the fly and I feel that a longer leader loses some of the suggestion which you intend to give. For example, you impart a smart foot-long pull and by the time that action is transmitted to the fly (on a longer leader) it is a half-hearted and uninspiring movement. Shorten the leader and you will observe how much more like the intended retrieve, it looks.

While I do not fancy a longer than 9 ft leader with a sinker, I have seen situations where a much shorter leader has claimed exclusive results. Admittedly, I refer once again to a New Zealand experience, but it does give one food for thought.

On a river such as the Tongariro which is extremely powerful, one of the basic rules for success is to get the fly down to the fish which, for the most part, hug the bottom. It is fascinating to watch a line of anglers proceeding carefully down to a pool and to note the solitary success of one of them. In the main, after the first success, the ubiquitous question "What fly?" will be asked and most will switch to that pattern. Yet the successful angler will continue triumphant.

Now, even on some of the more placid Tongariro pools, the standard gear will be a 9 weight lead-cored shooting head and, let's face it, if you're not dredging the bottom with that, you never will! But the secret is, if you're using a conventional leader, ie. six inches less than the rod length, the flyline might be getting down, perhaps even snagging, but your fly on its long leader is still sailing over the heads of the fish. The successful angler however has simply shortened his leader so that it is more at the mercy of the lead core and is within striking range of the fish. Sometimes the leader is shortened to 18 inches. Being so close to the flyline and yet achieving success makes one wonder just how aware trout are of our plastic lines. The other point to note is, how critical it can, at times, be to present the fly at the right depth. (Even in the shallower areas of the river, where floating line and nymph are utilised, the attachment of a dropper is sometimes necessary to achieve the same result. In some areas of New Zealand, leaded flies were not permitted).

I mentioned a possible exception where I might consider a longer than normal leader with a sinking line and this is in stillwater where a buoyant pattern such as a Muddler Minnow is being used. Using the Muddler is an extremely effective ploy in fishing different levels, if one is not sure where the fish are. The Muddler, on a sinking line, will float at the surface until the sinking line pulls it under, but it has no sinking qualities of its own to speak of. If dressed with a generous deer-hair head, it will remain either buoyant on the surface or if the water is deep, suspended somewhere in mid-water.

Having allowed the line to sink to the bottom, a retrieve can be initiated which will pull the Muddler down. On the pause of the retrieve, the in-built "floatability" of the pattern will cause it to try and rise to the surface. Thus a most attractive retrieve can be achieved.

The use of the longer leader can be to prevent the Muddler from being dragged totally into the weed by the submerged flyline. Instead it can be made to bob suggestively along just above the weed.

(d) RETRIEVING — IT'S ALL IN THE MIND

Ask any flyfisher and he will be able to recall a variety of occasions in which a trout took his fly: trout on a fast retrieve, a slow retrieve, a long pull, two short twitches. He will be able to recount instances where fish took the fly on the drop, motionless on the bottom, reeling in and so on.

It all adds up to a rather confused, seemingly meaningless jumble, which invites one to say that, in the end equation, it doesn't matter what retrieve is used.

Study a cross-section of our more experience anglers and it will appear as though each has his own favourite brand of retrieve. I have had a day when the three trout in the bag all took the fly when I had given up hope and was reeling in. Then I can recall a period on Plewman's Pond where the trout were careering after sedge. They didn't want a dry fly on the water; they didn't want it skittered along the surface; they wanted it half-drowned in the surface film and totally motionless.

The interesting aspect of that day was the manner in which they took the fly. Usually the text books will suggest that the faster the retrieve, the harder the take and vice versa. Well, these flies were small, defenceless and motionless, but, if I was fishing straight off the reel, ie. no slack, each trout would have caused a "smash take".

In general however, a great deal of attention should be paid to the retrieve, incorporating a certain amount of rhythm and a great deal of sensitivity. The rhythm is there as a sort of red warning light and the sensitivity is to extract every subtle advantage of movement out of the in-built suggestive qualities of the fly.

What is meant by rhythm? Any conventional retrieve, whether it be a pull, twitch or pluck incorporates a repetitive feature. In between, is the pause. In my experience the take is most commonly felt on the pause. If there is a certain rhythm involved, the angler (and the fish) can actually synchronise. Perhaps it is my imagination, but if I employ a jerky, out of time retrieve, I seem to get a snatching disjointed take, which usually results in a "short" take, ie. the fish is not hooked, or a lightly hooked fish.

To clarify, I can use a jerky retrieve providing there is a rhythm to it. The pause is the cue for the fish to commit and my own response on feeling the draw is to tighten up. Thus, if I feel the pull on the line, I simply pinch the line between thumb and forefinger on the rod holding hand. The trout, which has turned with the fly in its mouth, is hooked by virtue of this arresting movement. There is no sudden strike or any other impetuous action, just a stopping of the fly moving away.

What sort of retrieve should be used?

Essentially one's retrieve should, in the first place, be in accord with the type of fly used and therefore there are countless permutations which can be considered. I have found two useful standard retrieves which can cover most situations. On the sinker, a simple pull-pause technique, with the pause being slightly accentuated, is most effective. With a floating line, I prefer the double twitch. That is a twitch-twitch-pause method. What I like about this is that there is a delayed action. Many aquatic creatures have a double movement. The first is when they physically move, eg. kick and the second is the actual propelling as a result of the kick.

It's an extremely difficult task describing a good retrieve, but I find it helps to conjure up a mental picture of the fly and visualise how it should be moving with the retrieve you are using. If the picture doesn't convince you, it's certainly not going to convince the trout.

(e) BACK TO THE DRY FLY

The cult of the dry fly certainly knew how to maintain its preserve. From Halford's description of how it ought to be practised, it is no wonder that a mysticism has grown up about it. Imagine contemplating a situation in which the success of your mission involves identification of a female March Brown. The mind of the reader boggles and even the attempts of Skues to explode the fancy was not successful.

Yet one must, I believe, take care not to form too many parallels with dry fly fishing in general, and that which was in vogue on the chalkstreams. In South Africa, the use of the dry fly on stillwater is almost non-existent. Tom Sutcliffe, Hugh Huntley and Co, resort to it in Natal and one may find a loner in the Transvaal pottering around, but it is unusual to find a dry fly angler plying his trade.

Many Transvaal waters are simply not suited to the use of the floating fly. In general there is too much suspended silt reducing visibility. Then too, usually hatches of fly are sparse and sometimes extremely localised. These are the main negatives and yet the thought of using dry fly should not be excluded.

Certainly the scarcity of natural fly around does not worry me too much, but I do confess that I do like conditions to be right and the water to be clear.

What do I mean by conditions? The easiest way to describe it is to say that conditions should look as though there might be a hatch. A balmy sort of day, a touch of sun and a light breeze. An obvious spot to go for is off the windward bank putting the fly along the ripple where it meets the calm water. Sometimes one might find that the wind has driven food across to the opposite shore and there the trout are quietly feeding a foot or two out. One never really knows where the dry fly will be profitable for, in many instances, it is the proximity of food that can induce a trout out of his comfort zone, just long enough to sample a passing fancy. In extremely clear water, it is not unknown for trout to come up from great depths to take a fly off the surface and then dive back down again. One of the most patent examples of fish acutely attuned to scrutinising the surface for food is in the case of a shallow fast-flowing rocky stream. There may be no hatch of fly, but that does not prevent those river trout from taking a dry.

I can recall a morning on the Blyde near Pilgrims Rest. I had walked down to a run and stood for a while to observe any movement that might be taking place. There was nothing. No fish rising and I could not spot any fish. Nevertheless with my very light outfit, I started searching upstream with a small Irresistible. A quarter of an hour later I had released half-a-dozen fish. Small, certainly, but nevertheless an interesting exercise in realising that, even in the absence of a full scale rise, trout, accustomed to keeping an eye on the surface, will stir themselves.

In stillwater there is a lot more sub-surface food for the trout to occupy themselves with, yet I still believe that, if the water is clear, there is a great deal of scope.

Plewman's Pond in the Eastern Transvaal is a prime example of such a dam. Barely half an acre in extent, it has clarity, good weed growth and what is more, a good hatch of fly. As I write this, it has been designated a "floating line" only, which admittedly can translate into long-leader-leaded-pattern fishing, but with the regularity of rises, most people find it more productive to use a dry fly.

As with most small dams, one's approach to the water has to be cautious, but it affords one the opportunity of observing at close range the behaviour of the fish — and anglers.

Dry fly fishing in such circumstances requires a modicum of patience. For the most part, one spends some time observing and then stalking the fish. Once the fly has been put out, many anglers seem to think that if the fly is not taken instantaneously, the fish has gone. Presuming, of course, that my presentation did not spook the trout, I tend to leave the dry fly floating for quite some time. I do not retrieve at all, only taking up any slack that might eventuate. In most cases, there is no sudden rise as the fly hits the water and one must give the fish a chance to see the fly. Remember, if a trout is feeding near the surface, his "window" (area of vision) is quite small and it may take him a while to spot your dry.

Dry fly fishing can be exasperating at times, where one experiences a number of rises but no connections. A common explanation is that the trout are "coming short" and that they have refused the offering by turning away at the last minute.

There is another reason for this behaviour and the flyfisher can profit by this if he can control his desire to strike. The first clue to look for is in the rise itself. If it is a splashy or reasonably violent rise yet on striking there is nothing, it is most probable that the fish are not taking the fly at all, but are deliberately splashing it to "drown" it. It needs nerves of steel not to react and besides, one may get a genuine rise, so the easiest thing is to waterlog the dry fly so that, instead of floating on the surface, it lies in the surface, in the manner of a spent spinner.

This behaviour of the trout is very common if there is a hatch of sedge or any fast or erratically moving natural fly. The trout knows his prey is difficult to catch, so he forestalls any escape by splashing it. Once the sedge's wings are wet, it cannot get airborne and the trout can turn and take it in the surface film. So, if you can, watch closely and let the trout complete its antics. But beware, ten seconds later you'll get an almighty take, which can quite easily leave your leader flyless.

There are many patterns of dries on the market, but I personally carry along the Irresistible, D.D.D., Troutbeck Beetle and Tups Indispensable to cater for most of the conditions. With the exception of the D.D.D. where I might use a larger size, the range to take along are 12-16's.

Most anglers don't have the confidence to use a dry fly, but, one day, when the water is clear and the weather's reasonable, take out the dries and spend an hour.

You might just be surprised.

(f) POLAROIDING FOR TROUT

Part of the power of observation lies in looking for trout as one wanders along the banks. Some anglers have extremely good eyesight and are able to spot trout without using polaroids at all, but for the majority, this aid is essential.

It may seem trite to mention this, but polaroids are not simply dark glasses. An ordinary pair of sunglasses makes the surroundings appear darker; polaroids eliminate surface glare and allow the angler to see, in a clearer fashion, that which lies beneath the surface.

The second principle of trout spotting, even with the assistance of polaroids, is not to look for a fish. By this I mean, that it is highly unlikely that a whole fish outline will be seen at first glance. Unless a fish swims past under your nose, the probability is that, when scanning the water, your first impression will be either of movement or of shadow. This is particularly so in a stream. Our eyes are accustomed to focusing on an object, thus if one is scrutinising a deep clear pool in a river, the tendency is to focus on the bottom. You will clearly see every pebble that is there — but no trout. Stand for a while however, and you will find your eyes adapting. Then, perhaps a shadow moves, but even so, what is observed is no more than the shadow. The trout, a pale green almost translucent object is not lying on the bottom of the pool, but higher up in the water and depending on the sun, at an appropriate angle to the shadow. The shadow is a clue as to the whereabouts of the trout, but even with this knowledge, initially only a portion of the fish will be seen. Only with practice will a clearer outline be observed.

The art of spotting fish definitely comes with practice. I recall a day, looking down into the green depths of the Cliff Pool, Waitahanui River, when I proudly told my companion I could see trout there. Yes, he said, he could also see twenty-one. I didn't tell him I had only seen three. (A second scrutiny showed me 17 — never did find the other four). By the way, these weren't small fish either; their weights varied from 2-11 lbs.

In New Zealand rivers, one relies on the ability to spot fish to save time. Down South Island way, there are good fish to be had, but one might walk miles between each one, so it pays to develop these skills. I learnt a lesson on the famous Mataura one day. My friend consistently outspotted me and on one occasion he showed me an eight pound brown trout not six feet away which I still couldn't see. Eventually I made out a ghostly patch of white swinging gently from side to side. It was the big brown's tail sticking out from between some roots. I had, of course, been looking for a fish, not for a lighter piece of water.

Remember, it's easy to see fish after they have been scared, but the object is to catch them.

In stillwater the task is not quite so difficult, except that overall, the water is often pretty murky. Even so, a cautious walk along the bank or dam wall can pay dividends. Not so long ago, late in May, I had an occasion to drop into Kamberg. The water was absolutely perfect for polaroiding and a recce indicated a number of largish brown trout. For the most part, they were moving quickly which augurs poorly for angling, but eventually I found an unobtrusive corner where a brace of browns and half-a-dozen smaller rainbows were milling around. The fish were no more than a yard out so I did all my fishing sitting down. To limit casting activity I put out a small dry fly and watched an unobtrusive current push it slowly out into the dam. After a couple of false rises, there was a more determined take and a nice sized Brown came to net. (It was interesting watching the reaction of another group who were fishing with sinking lines. They watched our apparent inactivity with uncertainty at first, but after I hooked the Brown, we noticed them watching us with a pair of binoculars. Perhaps they thought we were up to no good!)

While polaroiding is useful for spotting trout, it can also help in two further circumstances. When fish are rising, it is possible to catch them, providing one knows in which direction they are moving. So often a cast is put down in the vicinity of the rise, but because the fish is so close to the surface, it is more than likely that the fly will be "ignored" simply because the trout is browsing off in another direction.

Another practical use comes into play at the end of a retrieve. Trout, especially big ones, are notorious for following a fly in. I am very careful at the end of each retrieve not to yank the fly out of the water, preferring to wait until I see the fly and whether it has a shadow behind it. In this way I can keep the retrieve going and even use a lift of the rod to induce a take. Of course, at this stage all the action is visible and it can be quite exciting to see a fish take the fly in front of your very eyes.

It should also be obvious that polaroids are useful in determining structure, eg. weedbeds and channels and this information is probably more important in the long run than in seeing individual fish.

IN CONCLUSION

Whether or not one regards choice of fly to be incorporated within the definition of presentation, there is no doubt in my mind that such selection process is important if one wishes to catch trout consistently. More experienced anglers will say that they could use one pattern to good effect for a great part of the season, but it is only by virtue of their experience that they could accomplish this. And even though success is achieved, there would be plenty of situations where they would yearn for the comfort of an alternative.

Yet it is not only the availability of a suitable selection that should be considered, for, as we have also discussed, the properties of any individual fly are crucial. Colour, form, movement and texture are all aspects which have been alluded to and which will help to deceive the trout.

A colleague of mine suggested that I should try to give a shortlist of flies for various occasions and this, within limitation, I suppose one could do, but it rather defeats the whole object of understanding the principle of "why" a particular fly should be chosen. There should be a reason for a decision, rather than a haphazard guess. Unfortunately guesswork is too often the order of the day. Because of a lack of understanding, many anglers do not catch the number of trout they deserve.

Neither am I an advocate of angling to see how many fish one can catch, for I believe that the catching of a trout, on most days is not a difficult task. With experience, one becomes au fait with well-tried methods and a resultant lack of challenge creeps in. It's not unusual for such experienced anglers to begin to limit or vary their methods of catching trout. It then becomes a quest, not for numbers of trout caught, but for a satisfaction in having accomplished the task by using a new method.

Have you ever watched an angler's face when he catches his first trout on a floating line, or on a dry fly or in a river. It is not the mere capture that is important; it is the achievement.

Yet, for the moment, our objective is to try and deceive more trout than previously and providing some thought is put into the exercise this can be accomplished.

In the end equation it's each man to his own, but I can promise you now, that to catch a trout is only the tip of the iceberg to be explored.